To Kill a Mockingbird

Harper Lee

Guide written by Stewart Martin

A Letts Literature Guide

Extracts from *To Kill a Mockingbird* by Harper Lee, published by William Heinemann, are reproduced by kind permission of Reed International Books.

First published 1994
Reprinted 1994, 1995, 1996

Letts Educational
Aldine House
Aldine Place
London W12 8AW
0181 740 2266

Typeset by Jordan Publishing Design

Self-test questions devised by Hilary Lissenden

Text Design Jonathan Barnard

Cover and text illustrations Hugh Marshall

Graphic illustration Ian Foulis and Associates, Barbara Linton

British Library Cataloguing in Publication Data
A CIP record for this book is available from the British Library.

ISBN 1 85758 262 4

Printed and bound in Great Britain by
Ashford Colour Press Ltd, Gosport, Hants

Letts Educational is the trading name of BPP (Letts Educational) Ltd

Contents

Plot synopsis

The story is set in the mid-1930s in Maycomb, a small, isolated, inward-looking town in Alabama, USA. The narrator is Scout Finch, who looks back to when she was a young girl living with her brother Jem and their father Atticus, a lawyer. Their household is looked after by Calpurnia, a stern but kind Negro woman, because the children's mother died when they were very young. At Scout's first day at school we meet some of the children of the long-established local families, like the Cunninghams and the Ewells.

Scout and Jem, together with their new friend Dill, try to get a mysterious neighbour who has not been seen for fifteen years – Boo Radley – to come out of his house. Atticus disapproves of their activities, because he is trying to bring his children up to be tolerant and he thinks they are pestering Boo. Although Boo has a frightening reputation amongst the local children, he leaves Scout and Jem presents hidden in a hole in a tree outside his house. During a cold winter night, a fire burns down their neighbour's home and, unknown to Scout, Boo puts a blanket round her shoulders to keep her warm.

Atticus is to defend Tom Robinson, a Negro man accused of raping a white woman. This causes tension with some of the white townspeople, many of whom are deeply prejudiced and racist. The children learn new respect for Atticus when he shoots a mad dog, and they discover that he is known in the town as an expert with a rifle.

As a punishment for destroying Mrs Dubose's camellias, Jem has to read every day for a month to this cantankerous dying neighbour. After Mrs Dubose's death, Atticus tells the children that she was a brave woman who died having won her painful fight with an addiction to painkillers. On a visit to Calpurnia's church, the children learn more about Tom Robinson.

Aunt Alexandra comes to stay. There are difficulties when she tries to make the children behave as she thinks proper and when she tries to get Atticus to sack Calpurnia. The trial of Tom Robinson takes place amidst strong feelings in the community, especially when Atticus demonstrates that Tom is probably innocent by questioning the girl, Mayella Ewell. It is clear that she has lied about the rape, but after long consideration by the jury, Tom Robinson is found guilty. The girl's father, Bob Ewell, spits at Atticus and threatens trouble in the future. Tom Robinson tries to escape from prison and is shot seventeen times.

On their way home from a Halloween pageant one dark night, the children are attacked with a knife by Bob Ewell and Jem is badly hurt. During the fight, Boo Radley comes to their aid and Bob Ewell is killed. The sheriff persuades Atticus to pretend that Bob Ewell fell on his knife.

Background to the novel

History plays such an important role in the novel in shaping the people's attitudes that it is useful to know some background. The American Civil War, which took place between 1861 and 1865, occurred when a group of Southern states, including Alabama, formed the Confederate States of America, and broke away from the main Union of States. After four years of bitter fighting they were defeated and rejoined the Union. One of the results of the Civil War was the end to black slavery. Although in theory the Negroes were equal to the whites, in fact most of them continued to live separate lives, reluctantly accepting their inferior status. The story is set in the 1930s, yet by this time – seventy years since the end of the war – the situation for Negroes had hardly changed. Negroes were still segregated. The position of the Negroes in the Southern states had begun to change at the time Harper Lee wrote the book (in the late 1950s), with civil disturbances and rioting proving that blacks were no longer prepared to accept the position of inferiors. The events in the book happen before the big Civil Rights movement, but after the Ku Klux Klan's activities had begun to die down. It is also a time of economic depression, which President Roosevelt was trying to improve with his 'New Deal' policy.

Maycomb is a small town in Alabama. Most of the population and that of the surrounding farming community are poor. The population has remained virtually unchanged for decades, with the result that newcomers are not accepted easily. Cars are few, cinemas non-existent. The people are very religious, mainly Baptist or Methodist. Everyone knows everyone else, and local gossip is rife. The Negroes are segregated and most white people want them to remain so. Anyone who does not conform to accepted patterns of normal behaviour, like Mr Radley or Dolphus Raymond, is regarded as an oddity. So little happens that major events such as the rape trial are regarded as a day out for the whole county. Maycomb is a 'tired old town' that is long overdue for a fresh breeze of change.

Characters and themes

Scout

A hot-tempered tomboy, who is six at the start of the book. She is the narrator of the story, which is about her childhood memories.

Jem

Scout's elder brother. He is ten at the start of the book.

Atticus

The father of Jem and Scout. He is a widowed lawyer who defends a Negro against an unjust accusation.

Dill

The close friend of Jem and Scout who comes to Maycomb each summer to stay with his aunt. He is nearly seven at the start of the book.

Boo Radley

Arthur (Boo) Radley

A mysterious man who stays inside his house. Nobody has seen him come out for fifteen years.

Calpurnia

Atticus' family cook, who exercises firm control over Jem and Scout, and acts as their mother.

Miss Maudie Atkinson

The elderly favourite neighbour of Jem and Scout, who treats them kindly and bakes them cakes.

Courage

There are many kinds of courage: physical (being brave); moral (standing up for what is right); and the courage needed to survive failure. The novel shows clearly how destructive it is to a person's character if they live their life without courage.

Family

The family – or 'background' - of a person is used by some characters to judge them by. In contrast, other characters (like Atticus) try always to judge a person by the content of their individual character.

Justice

The law says that in order for justice to be done all people must have equal rights. The novel explores the difficulties of making this work when people's attitudes and prejudices get in the way.

Prejudice and hatred

Several characters in the book display prejudice and hatred towards other people. This is shown to be destructive towards everybody – especially towards those people who hold such feelings for others.

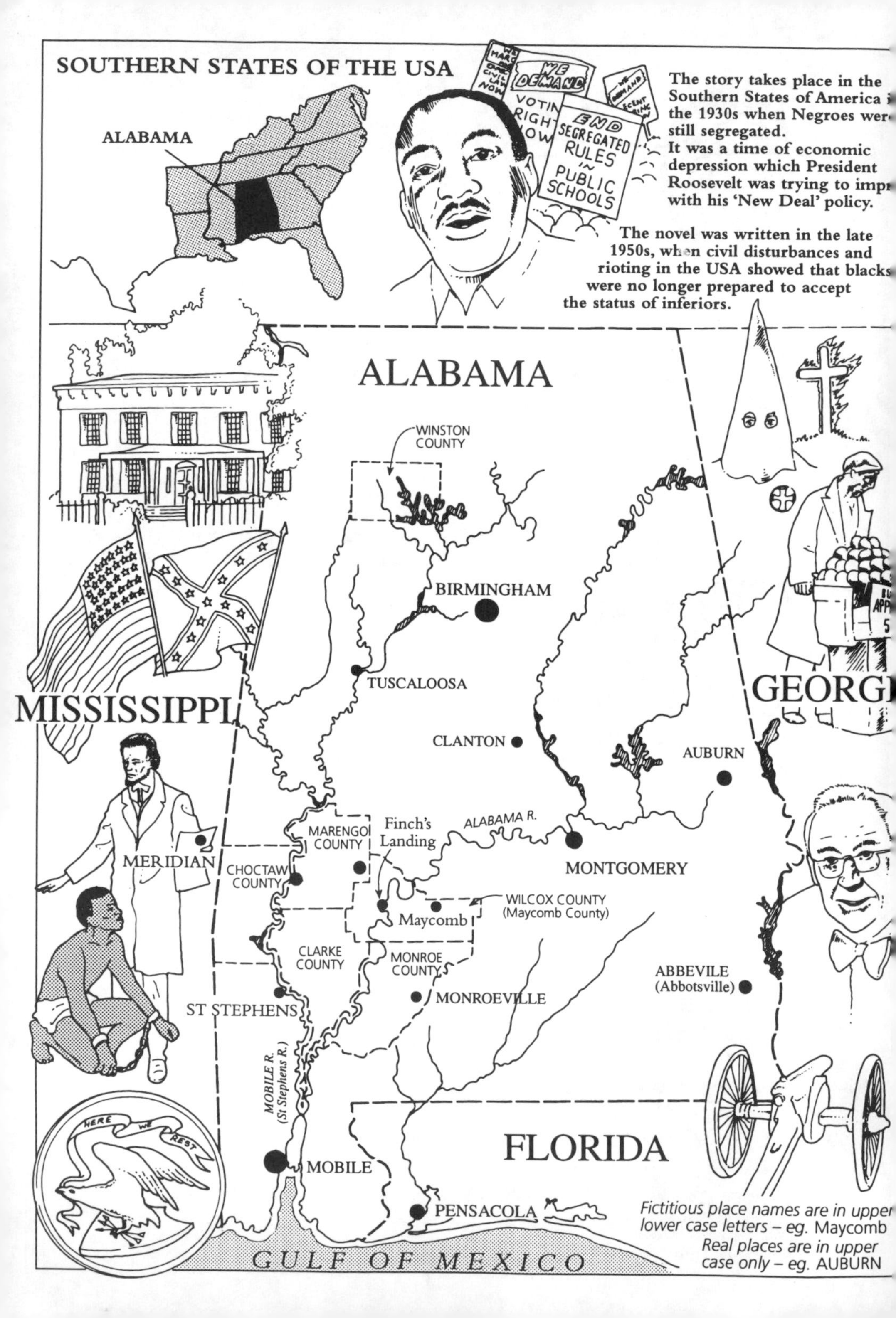
SOUTHERN STATES OF THE USA
ALABAMA
The story takes place in the Southern States of America i
the 1930s when Negroes were
still segregated.
It was a time of economic depression which President Roosevelt was trying to impr
with his 'New Deal' policy.
The novel was written in the late 1950s, when civil disturbances and rioting in the USA showed that blacks
were no longer prepared to accept the status of inferiors.
WE DEMAND
VOTING RIGHTS NOW
END SEGREGATED RULES IN PUBLIC SCHOOLS
ALABAMA
WINSTON COUNTY
BIRMINGHAM
TUSCALOOSA
MISSISSIPPI
GEORG
CLANTON
AUBURN
MARENGO COUNTY
Finch's Landing
ALABAMA R.
MONTGOMERY
MERIDIAN
CHOCTAW COUNTY
WILCOX COUNTY
(Maycomb County)
Maycomb
CLARKE COUNTY
MONROE COUNTY
ABBEVILE
(Abbotsville)
ST STEPHENS
MONROEVILLE
MOBILE R.
(St Stephens R.)
HERE WE REST
FLORIDA
MOBILE
PENSACOLA
GULF OF MEXICO
Fictitious place names are in upper
lower case letters – eg. Maycomb
Real places are in upper
case only – eg. AUBURN

1933
PART ONE
EARLY SUMMER
Dill arrives from Meridian. Jem and Scout decide to make Boo Radley come out of 'hiding'.
SEPT
Scout starts school with Miss Caroline. We meet fellow pupils, Walter Cunningham and Burris Ewell.
1934
SUMMER
Gifts appear in the tree. Dill returns for the summer, and the children keep trying to see Boo. The hole in the tree is filled with cement.
NOV 21ST
Tom Robinson is arrested.
WINTER
Miss Maudie's house burns down: Boo, unseen, wraps a blanket round Scout. Scout gets into fights when Atticus is accused of defending a Negro. Atticus explains about self-respect.
1935
SPRING
Atticus shoots a mad dog: Jem and Scout are surprised and proud.
The dying Mrs Dubose is rude about Atticus: Jem destroys her camellias. Atticus makes him read to her: he wants Jem to 'see what real courage is!'
1935
PART TWO
SUMMER
Jem and Scout go to the Negroes' church, where a collection is taken for Tom Robinson's family. Calpurnia explains that Tom is accused of raping Mayella Ewell.
Aunt Alexandra comes to stay and tries to 'improve' the children and get rid of Calpurnia. Dill arrives again, saying his parents do not want him.
Atticus tries to keep the Sarum mob from lynching Tom Robinson: Scout's innocent friendliness to Mr Cunningham brings them to their senses.
An obviously innocent Tom Robinson is found guilty at his trial, despite Atticus' defence, and Bob Ewell spits in the face of Atticus.
AUG
Tom Robinson is killed trying to escape.
OCT
Bob Ewell loses his job, blames Atticus, and makes trouble.
Bob Ewell is killed trying to hurt Scout and Jem. Their rescuer turns out to be Boo himself.

Who's who in *To Kill a Mockingbird*

Scout

The story is narrated by Scout, who is six years old at the beginning and nine when the story ends. The language of the book is adult in style, because Scout is recounting memories of her childhood. Interestingly, the book is set in the 1930s and Harper Lee would have been seven in 1933. She is therefore contemporary with Scout. Scout is a lively, intelligent, astute girl who prefers boyish activities. She has a strong will and a hot temper which gets her into trouble with adults. She dislikes school intensely and lets her feelings be known to the teacher. Scout has a close relationship with her father, who tries to make her use her head instead of her fists. Before the trial she is taunted by the other children because Atticus is defending a Negro. Her instinctive reaction is to fight back but, swallowing her pride, she obeys her father and refuses to retaliate. Scout's wild behaviour and frank speech offend Aunt Alexandra, who feels Scout should become more 'ladylike'. Scout resists these attempts to make her more feminine, preferring the openness of male company to the sly suggestions made by her aunt's companions.

Scout's character changes as she begins to learn how to look at things from another person's point of view. She learns to understand the feelings of Boo Radley and of her aunt, and also to respect the changes in Jem. She has great sympathy for Mayella Ewell and for her friend Dill, and is quite without prejudice. Having a child's mind and approach to life is often shown in the novel to be an advantage; the situation outside the court-house, when Atticus faces a lynch mob, is a good example of this. The children learn by experience that adults are not always right, and Scout illustrates the importance of developing an open and unprejudiced mind of one's own. She decides early in life that no matter how other people seek to divide up the human race into different sorts or types of people, there is really 'just one kind of folks. Folks.'

Jem

The story begins when Jem is ten and finishes when he is thirteen. The development of his character is traced as he approaches adolescence. At first, Jem enjoys normal childhood pursuits like playing football, inventing games, and amusing himself with his friends. As the story unfolds, Jem becomes more moody, is less willing to join in games with Scout and Dill, and prefers to be on his own. He is milder tempered than his sister Scout, and more sensitive to other people. Jem is four years older than Scout and this is reflected in his attitudes and reactions. The author uses the clever device of allowing us to see Scout trying to guess at Jem's thoughts on several occasions; this reveals a great deal about both Scout and Jem. A good example of this occurs in Chapter 7, when the children find the two carved soap figures in the Radley's tree.

Only on one occasion does Jem explode into anger – when he knocks off the tops of Mrs Dubose's camellias. As a result of this incident he learns a lot about personal courage. Tom Robinson's trial is also a very significant event in Jem's growing up. He is devastated by the unjust verdict and it takes him a long time to come to terms with the imperfection of people. At the same time his awareness of the feelings of others increases and he finally understands that Boo Radley stays indoors because he wants to, not for all the sinister reasons the children had imagined earlier. Jem develops a keen sense of responsibility, which is shown when he seems to break the childhood code of secrecy and informs Atticus of Dill's presence at the Finch house. He becomes more protective towards his sister, and develops a tactfulness and a way with words that reminds us of his father, Atticus.

Atticus

Atticus Finch, fifty years old and a widower, is the father of Jem and Scout. With the help of Calpurnia, the cook, he is raising the children on his own. He stands out as a man of reason and courage. In the face of the prejudice and strong emotions of the people of Maycomb he tries to make his own children see that it is better to use one's head than to resort to fists or, even worse, to guns. Atticus shows considerable bravery in defending Tom Robinson, knowing the likely unjust outcome of the trial. He is driven by a strong belief in the equality of people before the law, and although he fails this time to gain a just verdict it does not diminish his faith in the law for, as he remarks in Chapter 11: 'before I can live with other folks I've got to live with myself. The one thing that doesn't abide by majority rule is a person's conscience.'

His children are disappointed that Atticus doesn't play football or poker, and that he neither drinks nor smokes. Atticus is described as old and short-sighted. On the other hand, he is an expert marksman and a man to be relied upon. The people who matter in Maycomb hold Atticus in very high regard.

Atticus is subjected to criticism from his brother and sister because of the way he brings up his children. Although he gives Jem and Scout considerable freedom he demands high standards of courtesy, honesty and good manners from them. He is very fair with them and will always listen to both sides of any argument. He represents the voice of truth and fairness in the community – notice Dolphus Raymond's opinion of him in Chapter 20. Miss Maudie says of him, 'We trust him to do right.'

Atticus' philosophy of life is expressed early in the novel when he says to Scout: 'You never really understand a person until you consider things from his point of view...until you climb into his skin and walk around in it' (Chapter 3). Despite his virtues, Atticus is not unapproachable. He is a popular man with a keen sense of humour. But Atticus is not perfect. His faith in the goodness of people leads him to underestimate Bob Ewell, with almost fatal consequences. His other mistake, in thinking that they don't have lynch mobs in Maycomb, might also have resulted in death.

Dill

Dill

Dill – whose real name is Charles Baker Harris – is nearly seven at the start of the book and is the friend of Jem and Scout. He comes to stay each summer with his Aunt Rachel, a neighbour of the Finches. They like his ability to think up stories and imaginative games. It becomes apparent that his liking for fantasy hides an unhappy home life. Towards the end of Chapter 14, Dill describes the way his parents ignore him. Although he is bought all that he could wish for, he feels unloved and unwanted. Dill is upset by the trial of Tom Robinson and the outcome leaves him feeling disillusioned about adults. Jem sees injustice as a challenge and says he wants to become a lawyer, but Dill thinks it is pointless to fight against it. He wants to become a clown when he is older and just laugh at grown-ups. In Chapter 22 Aunt Alexandra calls Dill 'cynical', which means always believing the worst.

Arthur (Boo) Radley

Arthur Radley, or Boo as the children call him, is a figure of fear and mystery at the beginning of the story. He was locked in the house by his father for stealing a vehicle and then resisting arrest fifteen years before. He is a monster, ghost or 'haint' in the minds of the children. ('Haint' probably comes from the French 'hanté', which means haunted.) The children learn that when he was thirty-three years old he calmly stabbed his father in the leg with a pair of scissors and had to be locked up in the courthouse basement. The community's fear exaggerates his activities to include poisoning pecan nuts in the schoolyard, eating cats and squirrels raw, terrifying Miss Crawford by staring through her window at night, and killing azaleas by breathing on them.

Boo gradually emerges as a very different sort of person from the one the children imagine him to be. When items appear in the tree outside his house, the children realise he is leaving them gifts. When Jem has to abandon his torn trousers on the Radley fence, they reappear mended. When Scout is watching the fire at Miss Maudie's house, Boo covers her shoulders with a blanket. Boo's greatest act of kindness is in coming to Jem and Scout's aid when they are attacked by Bob Ewell, even though this involves Boo in killing a man with a knife. It is only then that they actually meet Boo for the first time. He is very different from the monster of their imagination, or the man described by Stephanie Crawford in Chapter 1. He is a gentle, quiet, and very shy man.

Calpurnia

Calpurnia is more than just the family's cook. She is a replacement mother. Her firm control over the children causes Scout to resent her. Atticus trusts and supports Calpurnia entirely. When Aunt Alexandra wants to get rid of her, he is firmly against it. Calpurnia is intelligent and is one of the few Negroes in Maycomb who can read and write. She leads a 'double life', partly amongst white people and partly at home with her fellow Negroes. The children are surprised when they learn that she talks differently amongst her own people. Calpurnia is very down to earth in her explanation of this. People have got to want to be educated themselves. You cannot force them. If they do not want it, there is no point flaunting your own education.

Miss Maudie Atkinson

Miss Maudie is the children's favourite neighbour. She is popular with them because she treats them with kindness and respect. She genuinely likes their company, bakes them cakes and, most importantly, does not talk down to them. Miss Maudie is a very individual character, who shows courage by holding views different from those of other people in Maycomb. When the strict sect of Baptists criticises her for growing flowers, she matches their biblical quotations with others from the same source. Miss Maudie is quite philosophical about losing her house in the fire and cheerfully carries on with life. She is critical about people's motives when they go to watch Tom Robinson's trial, calling it a 'Roman carnival.' She knows that at the trial a verdict of guilty is inevitable, but she sees grounds for optimism, even though she thinks the verdict is wrong. She explains to the children that a small step along the path to true justice has been taken. She has a sharp tongue and is not slow to use it when faced with the hypocrisy of the ladies at the missionary tea. Scout admires and respects her for this. Together with Atticus, Miss Maudie represents the voice of reason amongst all the fears and prejudices of the town. Her attitude towards hypocrisy can be guessed from the way she reacts in Chapter 24, when Mrs Merriweather criticises Atticus. Miss Maudie says acidly: 'His food doesn't stick going down, does it?'

Themes and images in *To Kill a Mockingbird*

Courage

Courage

We can recognise several kinds of courage in the book. There is the basic courage required to overcome childish fears, such as running past the Radley place, or returning there to fetch the trousers that Jem caught on the fence. Atticus shows the same kind of physical courage in facing the mad dog, even though he has a gun in his hand. A more difficult form of courage is the moral courage that Scout has to find in order not to retaliate when her friends call her father names. It is not easy to be made to look like a coward. The most difficult form of courage to possess is the courage to take on and carry through a task which is certain to end in failure. Atticus has to do this when he defends Tom Robinson. Mrs Dubose also chooses to do this, when she attempts to rid herself of drug addiction even though she knows she is dying and, in that sense, there is no point to her battle. She wins her fight, and Atticus calls her 'the bravest person' he knows. Atticus wants the children to realise that courage is not 'a man with a gun in his hand'.

Bob Ewell is a man totally without courage. Instead of facing Atticus alone, Bob Ewell tries to take revenge on his children, and even then he does not have the courage to face them in daylight, but strikes in the darkness.

Family

Family

Because of the static nature of the Maycomb population, the same families have lived in the area for nearly two hundred years. As a result, some people feel that each family seems to inherit particular characteristics. They can say that a Cunningham is always be trusted or a Ewell is always dishonest. This leads to social division: every family is categorised on a particular scale and it is important to mix with the 'right' family. Aunt Alexandra is particularly prone to this kind of snobbery. She tries to prevent the children playing with the Cunninghams because they lack 'background'. Atticus is against this kind of social classification, preferring to judge a person on individual merit.

The Cunninghams are a family of very poor farmers who live in Old Sarum in the north of the county. Their roles in the book are varied but significant: they act mainly as a contrast to the Ewell family. The Cunninghams never borrow what they cannot return and they pay their bills promptly, even if they have to pay in vegetables rather than money. They are quite independent of the State. The Cunninghams' son, Walter, is poorly educated and has bad manners but Scout eventually recognises (unlike her aunt) that these things are not important. Walter is essentially a good child, whose circumstances have prevented him from learning to behave any differently.

It is thanks to a Cunningham that the lynch mob disperses at the jail. Scout recognises Mr Cunningham and by talking to him about family matters, she makes him think like an individual again and not like a member of a mob. Finally, thanks to another Cunningham, the jury is delayed in returning their verdict. This delay gives both Atticus and Miss Maudie grounds for optimism for the future of their society.

Justice

Justice

In theory, all American Negroes have had equal rights in law since the end of the Civil War in 1865. Yet that does not always mean they receive justice. The court's verdict against Tom Robinson, shown through Jem's trusting, inexperienced eyes, emphasises this. Atticus upholds his belief in the law for, apart from minor improvements which he agrees could be made, he thinks it is satisfactory. What do need to change are people's attitudes. The law can function, but justice cannot be carried out until attitudes change. It is people who must apply the law justly.

Judge Taylor is an honourable man who does his best to see that Tom Robinson has a fair trial by appointing Atticus to defend him. He is a responsible judge who keeps his court well disciplined, despite his casual air and unusual habits, such as eating cigars and cleaning his nails whilst the court is in session.

Prejudice

Prejudice and hatred

The deep hatred and fear that exists between Whites and Negroes means that violence could break out at any time. Look how the lynch mob, made up of normally reasonable, respectable men, are ready to kill and how they nearly succeed. Bob Ewell's hatred of Atticus nearly results in the death of Jem and Scout. Although circumstances force him to use his gun, Atticus does not want his children to admire violence. By pleading for tolerance, Atticus hopes to show the children how the causes of violence can be removed. Atticus is perhaps too idealistic here, because he misjudges the extent of Bob Ewell's hatred. In the same way, any hope that the racial problems of the South could be solved by tolerance alone was perhaps too optimistic.

A dominant theme in the novel is the cruelty that people inflict upon others by the holding of pre-formed ideas, 'the simple hell people give other people', as Dolphus Raymond puts it. These ideas are not simply deep racial prejudice, but also the intolerant, narrow, rigid codes of behaviour that the townspeople of Maycomb wish to impose on each other. This bigotry (another word for prejudice) is made all the more menacing by being depicted as 'normal' behaviour by many characters in the book. Against this background, people such as Boo Radley, Dolphus Raymond and, to some extent, Maudie Atkinson, are persecuted because they do not conform. Tom Robinson is found guilty even though it is strongly suspected that his accusers are lying, because he went against the 'acceptable' behaviour of a Negro and dared to feel sorry for a white person.

So deeply entrenched is racial prejudice in Maycomb that the townspeople do not realise their own hypocrisy. The author highlights such double standards during Aunt Alexandra's missionary circle tea. The women talk with great sympathy about the plight of the poor Mruna tribe in Africa, but later condemn the dissatisfaction of the Negroes in their own town. At school Miss Gates extols the virtue of American democracy, then complains that the Negroes are 'getting way above themselves'. Mr BB Underwood, editor of the *Maycomb Tribune*, despises blacks but also hates injustice. In contrast, Atticus is the personification of honesty, 'the same in his house as he is on the public streets', as Miss Maudie observes.

The Radleys' house is an endless source of fear and fascination to the children. They hear frightening tales of what has happened to Arthur, the son, since he has been kept locked in the house. When Arthur Radley got into trouble at the age of eighteen his father, a very strict Baptist, undertook to punish his son himself, rather than let the law do it. Since this incident, Mr Radley has not mixed with his neighbours.

Dolphus Raymond is also regarded as an oddity in the town, because he is a white man who chooses to live amongst Negroes. He is a sensitive man who loathes the society which makes black and white people live separately. Interestingly, the blacks in *To Kill a Mockingbird* do not seem to consider rebelling; the most that happens is that they become 'sulky'. They resent Tom's conviction but as they have been second-class citizens from birth, they seem to expect it. Does this make the way they are treated 'right'? Why do you think people persecute others? Is it because they are full of hate, or because they feel threatened?

The mockingbird

The image of the mockingbird occurs frequently in the book. The children are warned that it is a sin to kill this bird because all it does is sing. The mockingbird has no original song of its own, but merely copies the songs of other birds – hence its name. Both Tom Robinson and Boo Radley can be compared with this bird. They are both gentle people who have done no harm but only try to help others. Both their lives are distorted versions of what might have been 'normal', but for their individual circumstances and backgrounds. Like the mockingbird, Tom and Boo should be protected and cared for. Instead, they are hunted down by the mob, who are full of false courage, ignorance and shallow pride – like the children who shoot songbirds. Both Tom and Boo are persecuted, one by the jury and the other by the children and the gossips. The mockingbird symbol links to two important themes in the book: justice and childhood. Justice is 'killed' when the jury follow their own prejudices and ignore the true evidence. The innocence of childhood dies for Jem, Scout and Dill when they realise that the adult world is often a cruel and unjust place.

Text commentary

Chapter 1

The story is narrated by Scout, a young girl who lives with her father Atticus, her brother Jem, and their cook Calpurnia in Maycomb, Alabama, USA. This chapter introduces Dill, the friend with whom Scout and Jem share adventures, and the mystery surrounding Arthur Radley (whom the children call Boo). The children try to make Boo come out of his house.

'When he was nearly thirteen...'

The narrator's age at the time of the story is important, because it allows the novel to take advantage of two different viewpoints which are years apart, and this gives a more complete picture of events.

There is a strong sense of **autobiography** in the writing of this novel. The device of an older person retelling incidents from their childhood is not uncommon in literature, and it is used in *To Kill a Mockingbird* to good effect in two ways. Often Scout relates incidents that she does not fully understand, as happens in the case of Boo Radley, when Jem grasps – long before she does – that the items in the tree are presents from him to them. The reader can piece things together which Scout does not understand: this adds depth to the narrative. Scout's incomprehension also adds an element of humour. The second strength of looking at the story through a child's eyes is the impact it lends to the question of racial prejudice in the South. The injustice stands out because the children are aware of it for the first time.

Because the story is written almost exclusively from a **child's point of view**, very little is emphasised. Scout's style is flat and matter-of-fact, out of keeping with her youthful, impulsive approach to life. Some scenes read as though written partly with a cinema adaptation in mind.

'I said if he wanted...'

Atticus was named after a Roman who lived from 109–32 BC. The Roman Atticus escaped to Greece during the Roman civil war. He refused to join

either side in the civil war. Why is this an apt name for the children's father? Look at Chapter 16 to get an idea of why this might be.

Read this part of Chapter 1 carefully. Look at the map of Alabama on pages 8–9 and work out where you think Finch's Landing and Maycomb could be.

'During his first five...'

The importance of heredity and 'background' is a theme which runs throughout the book. We know that the Finch family have lived in this area for over a century. So strong is the family network that different families have become recognisable by definite characteristics. Thus the Haverfords are all jackasses, and the Cunningham and Ewell families have particular identities. How precise do you think these thumb-nail sketches are? This tendency to 'pigeon-hole' people is a part of the intolerance displayed by some characters in the novel.

To understand the behaviour of the people of this small southern town we need to feel the atmosphere of the place. **Maycomb** is a tired town: the pattern of life has not changed for a long time and there is no desire for change. It is hot, so life proceeds at a slow pace. It is poor, so there is no money to change or improve things. Most importantly, it is a town turned in on itself with no interest in the outside world.

What does all this tell you about the likely attitudes of its inhabitants? Would you expect them to be narrow-minded or broad-minded? Notice how the children at the school have already acquired the values of their parents, and how it is this which causes their new teacher so many problems. Do people who are intolerant usually come from backgrounds where the adults are prejudiced also?

'People moved slowly then'

The mid-1930s was a time of economic depression in America, especially in the South. The only hope that things might improve came from Franklin D Roosevelt, elected President in 1932, who offered Americans a 'New Deal'.

'Calpurnia was something...'

Although she is employed as the cook, Calpurnia's role in the family is obviously more important than that. What is Atticus' attitude to Calpurnia? Judging from the narrator's comments that Calpurnia's hand was 'wide as a bed slat...' and that she was 'tyrannical', what do you think she was like with the children? How do the children regard her?

"I'm Charles Baker Harris..."

Look at the direct way in which the children speak to each other. What particular qualities of the behaviour of children is the author conveying here? Consider what they say to each other about the subject of reading. What does Jem's remark, 'don't have any picture shows here' reveal about the backwardness of the town?

> The importance of **religion** in the lives of the people of Maycomb is significant in the book, and it is interesting that Jem should point out that the only picture shows they ever get in Maycomb are 'Jesus ones'. Is there any relationship between people's attitude towards religion and their attitude towards prejudice? Would it be fair to say that the most devoutly religious people tend also to be the most intolerant?

'Inside the house lived a...'

The mystery of the Radley Place is not sensed merely by the children. It becomes, for adults too, the object of superstition and fear. The townspeople of Maycomb are shown to be more influenced by fear than by reason.

'The misery of that house...'

The Radleys are regarded as strange and different because they do not conform to the rigid patterns of behaviour that the Maycomb people expect. Try to decide how far this is the fault of the Radleys, and how far it is the fault of the people of Maycomb.

What do you think of Mr Radley's behaviour towards his son Arthur? Is it in keeping with what you already know of the family that he should decide to deal with the trouble himself? Mr Radley is described as a man who 'took the word of God as his only law'. Can you understand how he can behave so cruelly to his son and yet profess to be religious?

'Nobody knew what form...'

The innocence of childhood is shown in the way Jem thinks that Boo Radley must be chained to the bed to make him stay in all those years. Atticus' experience of life and people tells him that there are 'other ways of making people into ghosts'. What sort of pressure do you imagine Boo's father and brother might have exerted on him to make him stay inside?

The use of the word 'ghost' is significant. Ghosts are believed in only by superstitious people. The children talk about Boo Radley as being a 'haint' (ghost). Is this only because he hasn't been seen for so long, or is there some other reason? Is there anybody, or anything, else in the novel that is made into a 'ghost' by the people of Maycomb?

"There goes the meanest..."

The cruelty of Mr Radley towards his son is underlined by Calpurnia's comment. Why is her condemnation of Mr Radley particularly significant? (Why do the children feel so surprised by her remark?) This is the first comment on the relationship between Negroes and Whites. What do we immediately learn of the position of the Negro? Why should it be that Calpurnia so rarely comments on the ways of *white* people?

'Jem gave a reasonable description...'

Read Jem's description of Boo. It is a wonderful combination of imagination and reason. Children are credulous and will believe stories as long as the stories seem plausible and agree with what the children already think. How true is this also of some of the adults in the novel? Think about the reactions of people at Tom Robinson's trial.

There is some rivalry between Jem and Dill. What does Dill say that finally makes Jem put 'honour' before 'his head'?

Chapter 2

Scout's first day at school does not go smoothly. She is scolded for knowing how to read and write, and for speaking out in Walter Cunningham's favour. The morning ends with her standing in the corner, her hands slapped. Harper Lee gently makes fun of an education system which is in favour of new methods, but which takes little account of individual abilities. The difficulties of being an outsider in a small town like Maycomb are emphasised when Miss Caroline Fisher (the new teacher) is given a hard time.

'Jem condescended to take me...'

Jem and Scout are very close but, according to Jem, once they are at school their friendship must stay private. Like many children, Jem feels he must conform in public to the behaviour of his friends. There is no room for his sister, a girl four years his junior, in his circle of school friends. The pressure to conform can also be seen in the behaviour of the adults in the book. Only individuals with strong consciences, like Miss Maudie and Atticus, can free themselves from it.

'Miss Caroline printed her name...'

Look at the strong influence of past events on people's attitudes. Miss Caroline Fisher is regarded with suspicion because of her origins; she comes from a part of Alabama that stayed loyal to the North during the Civil War. People have long memories – the story takes place over seventy years after the Civil War. North Alabama is seen as somewhere quite different from Maycomb because it is industrial, Republican and – most significantly – because people there have no 'background'.

Family

Miss Fisher's 'foreignness' is emphasised by her choice of story. She does not appreciate that the majority of her children come from a background that makes them 'immune to imaginative literature'. The word 'immune' is amusing and shows that the people of Maycomb regard some things as so foreign, so threatening to their way of life, that they are comparable with disease.

'I suppose she chose me...'

Justice

Harper Lee pokes fun at the public education system here, where a teacher scolds a child for having already learnt to do what it is her job to teach her. Miss Fisher behaves absurdly by telling Scout to stop her father teaching her, because it will interfere with her reading. Scout's sense of fairness is outraged because she does not understand what wrong she has done, especially as no one has really ever taught her to read.

"Don't worry, Scout..."

Harper Lee gently mocks Miss Fisher's faith in this new method of teaching. Jem is mistaken about it – the Dewey Decimal System is a popular method of classifying library books. The rigidity of the school system is shown when Scout is told she must print, not write, for the next two years. In all, Scout is not impressed with her first day at school. Are you?

> The author is critical of the **formal education** the children get at school and the way the system totally ignores their needs and abilities. Miss Fisher is new to Maycomb and unfamiliar with local customs. Some of the children give her a hard time because of this. She clings fixedly to her theories of education, without regard to the realities of the classroom. Hence her silly request that Scout must unlearn all she already knows about reading and writing and 'begin reading with a fresh mind'. The lessons about current events falter because the majority of children come from homes where the newspaper contains few 'current events'.

'I rose graciously...'

Family

Why does Scout think that the mention of Walter's surname will make everything clear? She perhaps assumes that everybody in the world is like the people of Maycomb. This is a normal attitude in children but is also that of many of the Maycomb adults.

'My special knowledge...'

The Cunninghams are proud, honest, poor and very independent. They will not accept charity from the church or government, in contrast to the Ewells, who gladly receive help from the state. Part of the humour in the book stems from Scout's innocent enquiries and statements. Here Jem teases her about the meaning of the word 'entailment'. (This is a legal term. It describes how land is settled on people other than the original owner so that no single person is the absolute owner of that land any more.) Scout obviously remembers the term – see Chapter 15.

> We gain an insight here into the plight of the **poor farmers in the South** during the 1930s. Poverty forced them to mortgage their property or sign entailments. This meant they then needed hard cash to repay debts. The government offered work in the form of paid welfare schemes, but taking the work meant they would have to leave their farms. People such as the Cunninghams, who were a 'set breed of men', were reluctant to do this because it would mean seeing their property go to ruin.

'Miss Caroline stood stock...'

This is another example of humour arising from Scout's innocence and ignorance. She makes an incorrect assumption about why she has to put out her hand. What do you think of Scout's behaviour on this, her first morning at school? Has she been outspoken, or is she merely unaware of the behaviour expected of her? Whose fault is it really that she is punished? In a more serious form, this might have been what happened to Boo Radley when he was young. Whose fault is it that Boo has ended up the way he has?

Scout

Family

'When Miss Caroline threatened...'

Think about whether you have any sympathy for Miss Caroline and try to decide why school has been so difficult on the first morning. Is it simply that she is new to the school? To what extent do you think her problems are caused by her not being from Maycomb, but from Winston

County, in North Alabama? It is clear that Miss Blount, a native Maycombian, seems to have certain advantages over her. How tolerant is Miss Caroline of the children of Maycomb? How tolerant is Maycomb of Miss Caroline?

Chapter 3

Burris Ewell arrives for his annual day of attendance at school, and Miss Fisher finds out about his 'cooties'. Walter Cunningham visits the Finch home for lunch and Scout is taught an important lesson by Calpurnia about politeness to guests. Scout also learns about the Ewells in Maycomb. The Ewells are a family for whom the normal rules of behaviour are relaxed, in order to shield the Ewell children from some of the bad habits of their 'contentious' father. Atticus tries to teach his children tolerance and to see things from the other person's point of view.

'Catching Walter Cunningham...'

Scout

The difference in temperament between brother and sister is quite marked. Scout is hot-headed, and settles arguments quickly in the only way she knows – with her fists. Jem is more reasonable. Look for similarities between Jem and his father. As Atticus is a widower, we cannot look for similarities between Scout and her mother. Unlike Jem, Scout does not remember her mother clearly. So who do you think Scout becomes more like as she grows up?

'Jem seemed to have little...'

The repartee between Jem and Scout is often very amusing. With the normal childlike desire for fairness and honesty, neither will let the other get away with boasting, invention or lies. Look at how Scout deflates Jem's claims about his behaviour in front of the Radley Place.

'While Walter piled food...'

One of the greatest lessons that Atticus and Calpurnia try to teach the children is tolerance of other people's behaviour. That is why Scout is so soundly scolded here.

Burris Ewell and Walter Cunningham are dressed very differently. Burris' clothes are filthy; Walter's are at least clean, if patched. The description of Burris's father as 'right contentious' (argumentative) is a forewarning of the dangers ahead. (See Chapters 23 and 28.)

Justice

'Atticus sat down...'

The need to look at circumstances from the other person's point of view is a strong theme in the book. It is the chief lesson Atticus teaches his children. He tries to make Scout see the day at school from Miss Caroline's point of view.

"Let us leave it at this,..."

Notice the Ewell family's characteristics. Atticus points out that for three generations, the Ewells have been 'the disgrace of Maycomb'. The law is bent for the Ewell children, out of compassion. Why is this more possible in a small town than it might be in a big city? Think about how everyone knows everyone else's business in a small town, and how this can lead not only to arrogance but also to humanity and compassion. (Look at what Reverend Sykes says to his congregation about Helen Robinson in Chapter 12.) How true is it that to know someone is to understand them, as Atticus seems to believe? The Bible suggests that to understand is to forgive. At the end of the novel we might be able to forgive Mayella Ewell, but can we forgive her father? Does Atticus forgive Mr Ewell, do you think?

Family

Chapter 4

A whole year passes, and Scout is disenchanted with school life. The mystery of the Radley place deepens as the children begin to find small gifts left in a tree outside. As yet, Scout does not suspect that these come from Boo. Dill arrives, and the children invent a new game re-enacting the drama of Boo Radley's life. Scout rolls inside a tyre into the Radley's garden. Afterwards, Scout is apprehensive, partly because she senses that Atticus disapproves of their game, partly because – unknown to the boys – she heard laughter coming from behind a shutter at the Radley Place.

'The remainder of my schooldays...'

The change in the author's style tells us that it is Scout the older person who is talking now. No child of six, however much she felt the boredom of school, could express herself in such a way. Knowing Scout's background, why would formal education be of so little use to her? She observes that 'Atticus and my uncle, who went to school at home, knew everything'.

The suspense about the Radley Place is kept alive by references to Scout and Jem running past the door as fast as possible. A new development now comes with the appearance of chewing gum in a hole in the tree outside.

Scout

'Finders were keepers...'

Do you think Jem has connected the Indian-heads (one cent coins) with Boo Radley? Here is an interesting gap between Scout the narrator, who understands the situation, and Scout the seven-year-old, who does not. Scout observes that, 'Before Jem went to his room, he looked for a long time at the Radley Place'.

Jem

'Two days later Dill...'

Dill enjoys the superior position that travel and life in a bigger town give him. He boasts, too, of his father's position. However, Jem and Scout are not taken in by him. Why does Dill make up so many tales about his parents, his travels and his life in general? Is Dill essentially a lonely child?

> What is the effect of saving until the end of the chapter the information that Scout heard someone laughing inside the Radley place? Scout's revelation suddenly adds drama and new meaning to something which has already happened in the novel. An important quality of the **author's style** is the way in which events assume a greater and often a different importance, the further we read. You, the reader, constantly change your understanding of things which happen, just like the children do. This technique – of revealing new slants on past events as time goes by – is also a skilful way of suggesting that the children are growing up.
>
> In a way, the book is **circular** in its construction; when you have finished reading it, try going straight back to the start and beginning again. Notice how the continuity of the story is maintained.

Chapter 5

Scout, having been edged out of the boys' games for a while, spends her time with Miss Maudie Atkinson. Miss Maudie is their friendliest neighbour, kind and generous to the children. She is critical of the local gossip, Miss Crawford, and of religious bigots like Mr Radley. She has tremendous sympathy for Boo Radley, whom she feels has been cruelly treated. The children's last attempt to communicate with Boo fails when Atticus catches them using a pole to push a note through one of the Radley's shutters. He forbids them to torment Boo any more, and urges them to look at their behaviour from Boo's point of view.

'Dill was in hearty...'

The humour at the start of this chapter lies in the straightforward way Scout relates events and deals with situations. She still is very much the young child who feels that any argument can be settled with fists. She gradually grows away from this idea as she matures.

'Miss Maudie hated her house...'

Miss Maudie is sympathetic towards the children. She allows them a great deal of freedom in her garden, talks to them in a friendly way, and offers them cakes. She is contrasted with the frightening, intolerant Mrs Dubose and the gossipy and rather empty-headed Miss Stephanie Crawford.

The strict sect of Baptists that Mr Radley belongs to had quite an influence in the South. Their narrow views about good behaviour add to the already intolerant atmosphere of Maycomb, and Scout seems to grasp intuitively that these strict Baptists must be wrong in condemning Miss Maudie to hell for loving her garden. Scout appreciates Miss Maudie's goodness, even though she does not actually go about 'doing good' in public, as some characters do.

'Miss Maudie stopped rocking...'

Miss Maudie's common sense makes her aware of the dangers of interpreting the Bible too literally. She fears that people like Mr Radley, who believe that they must strictly obey the laws of their religion, are hurting other people in the process. That, to her, is wrong. She says that these people are, 'so busy worrying about the next world they've never learned to live in this one...'.

Think about whether this criticism could be made of Mr Radley, Miss Stephanie Crawford, Mrs Merriweather, or Atticus. Miss Maudie's comment is a central argument in the novel, and that is why Harper Lee shows us so much of the children's education. The children learn to 'live in this world' in a way which many adults in the novel cannot. The educational system in Maycomb, as represented by the children's teachers, seems based on the assumption that 'projects' and 'units' are a good preparation for 'this world'.

"Do you think they're true...?"

Miss Maudie's nature is tolerant. She is critical of Miss Crawford for spreading rumours about Boo Radley. She looks upon Boo with sympathy, and sees his fate as the tragic result of his father's strict following of religious principles.

"You reckon he's crazy?"

Atticus' lack of hypocrisy is emphasised by Scout and Miss Maudie agrees: 'Atticus Finch is the same in his house as he is on the public streets'. How many other people in the book are like Atticus, as regards their public and private behaviour? Look at the list below. For each person, or group, decide whether you think they would be the same in private as they are in public, or different: Miss Maudie Atkinson, Miss Stephanie Crawford, Mrs Dubose, Mr Ewell, Mayella Ewell, Tom Robinson, the lynch mob (who appear in Chapter 15).

"You all've gone crazy..."

Why does Dill need to invent so many stories about his life? How do you think Dill's home life differs from that of Jem and Scout? Does this give you a clue about the reason he invents his stories?

Again Atticus tries to teach the children about tolerance and understanding. He urges them to look at what they have been doing from Boo Radley's point of view.

Chapter 6

Despite Atticus' ban, the children try a final time to make contact with Boo Radley. They go at night, and catch sight of a shadowy figure in the Radley backyard. Before they can discover its identity, the sound of Nathan Radley's gun frightens them off the premises. As they escape, Jem loses his trousers on some barbed wire. It takes all Dill's quick wits to make up a possible reason for their disappearance – he says that he beat Jem at strip-poker. Jem, fearing Atticus' anger more than Mr Radley's shotgun, goes back that night to retrieve his trousers. He finds them mended and hanging neatly on the fence.

'In the glare from...'

In this strictly religious atmosphere, what do you think would be people's attitude towards gambling? Look at Miss Rachel's reaction. The gentle humour of the book surfaces again in Scout's innocent misunderstanding of the reactions of adults – because they all 'stiffen' she thinks that 'the neighbours seemed satisfied' with Dill's outrageous explanation.

Chapter 7

Jem shows that he is more sensitive and mature than his sister. He guesses that Boo Radley repaired his trousers and hung them on the fence. He also suspects that the gifts in the tree (some twine, and soap carvings of two figures) are from Boo Radley. Jem's suspicions are confirmed when Boo's brother Nathan cements up the hole – sadly, before Jem can write a thank-you note. The knowledge that Nathan wants to prevent any friendship between Boo and the children reduces Jem to tears. Scout has not understood where the presents have come from or the significance of the cement, yet the narrator (the older Scout) is able to convey Jem's understanding to us at the same time as she illustrates Scout's ignorance.

'Jem stayed moody and silent...'

Scout is beginning to learn the lesson that Atticus has been teaching her. We do not yet know, however, why Jem is so moody. Scout assumes that it is a reaction to the terrifying experience of going back, alone, to the Radley Place at night. It is another example of how the reader does not yet know all the facts of every incident.

'One afternoon...'

How is Scout's behaviour in keeping quiet rewarded? Notice what the mended trousers make Jem realise about Boo Radley and about who is leaving the things in the tree. Why does this confuse him so much?

Jem is going through the painful process of discarding youthful assumptions and ideas which he has now discovered to be quite wrong. This is something which Atticus, amongst others, is trying to persuade the people of Maycomb to do – to discard their prejudice. Jem's inner development and growth is set in ironic contrast to the children's state education, whose achievements (teaching Jem about the Dewey Decimal System, and enabling him to walk 'like an Egyptian') seem wholly irrelevant to the real business of growing up.

Notice how the **narrator**, although the same person as Scout, can make Scout appear ignorant of the facts that the reader can guess at. This style of writing is relaxed but revealing, with a strong **story-telling flavour** to it. It is an engaging approach to adopt and is suitable for a novel like this, which moves from incident to incident and contains a lot of conversation mixed with description. This enables the writer to draw the reader right into the centre of the action.

'Less than two weeks later...'

Jem does not want Atticus to know where they found the things. Think about Atticus' reaction to their attempts to make Boo come out. Which things has Scout still not connected?

Jem realises that Mr Nathan Radley was lying about the tree. He had blocked it up deliberately. Think about why he might have done this and why it moves Jem to silent tears. Jem seems to understand more about what has been going on than his sister. This is another skilful touch by the author which reminds us of the different levels of maturity of the two children. It will help you to understand Jem's reaction if you think about what Dolphus Raymond says in Chapter 20 about the way people treat each other.

Self-test (Questions) Chapters 1–7

Uncover the plot

Delete two of the three alternatives given, to find the correct plot. Beware possible misconceptions and muddles.

Jean-Louise (Dill/Boo/Scout) and her brother John/Jem/Jack live with their father, Atticus, and their cook, Caroline/Maudie/Calpurnia, in Maycomb County, Alabama. It is the 1830s/1930s/1960s, and slavery/prejudice/economy, both racial and class-conscious, rages strongly. While Atticus practices criminal law/economy/tyranny the children spend their time at school and at play with their friend Walter/Burris/Dill. Their favourite game involves acting out the life of Arthur/Nathan/Chuck (Boo) Radley, a neighbour who has been shut away/dead/ill for so long that superstition surrounds him. As the game progresses (with Atticus' delight/disapproval/amusement) it becomes apparent that it is not going unnoticed by someone on the Finch/Crawford/Radley estate. During a night visit to the house, Jem loses his trousers: when he collects them they have been burned/stolen/folded and inexpertly darned. Small gifts are left in the knot-hole of a Radley oak, until Atticus/Boo's father/Boo's brother – claiming that the tree is dying – fills the hole with cement.

Who? What? Why? When? Where? How?

1. What does Scout think caused her father's 'profound distaste' for the practice of criminal law?
2. Where does Dill come from, and why does he come to Maycomb?
3. In what ways were the Radleys alien to Maycomb's ways?
4. How did Arthur's father view his son's sentence, and what was the result?
5. What can Scout do that – according to Miss Caroline – she shouldn't?
6. Who are 'the disgrace of Maycomb', and why?
7. How does Miss Maudie remember Arthur Radley?
8. What does Mr Radley 'shoot' in his collard patch?
9. When does Scout think she and Jem first began to part company, and why?
10. Why does Jem cry when Atticus says that the tree filled up by Mr Radley is not dying?

Who is this?

1. Who 'was all angles and bones; she was near-sighted; she squinted; her hand was wide as a bed slat and twice as hard'?
2. Who 'habitually pulled at a cowlick in the centre of his forehead'?
3. Who 'was a thin leathery man with colourless eyes'?
4. Who 'never took anything off anybody'?
5. Who, according to Miss Maudie, 'is the same in his house as he is on the public streets'?
6. Who was 'a chameleon lady who worked in her flower beds in an old straw hat and men's coveralls,...'?
7. Who said: 'If he wanted to come out, he would', and of whom?
8. Who said: 'Don't you cry, now, Scout... don't cry now, don't you worry'?

Names and nicknames

1. Why do Scout, Jem and Dill call Arthur Radley 'Boo'? Does the nickname have any particular effect(s), do you think?
2. 'We were far too old to settle an argument with a fist-fight, so we consulted Atticus. Our father said we were both right.' Atticus' name is very appropriate. Why? How does this quote illustrate Scout's (and Jem's) attitude to their father?
3. Jean-Louise's nickname is 'Scout'. There is no reference to or explanation of this in the text: do you think it expresses her personality or describes her actions in any way?

Self-test (Answers) Chapters 1–7

Uncover the plot

Jean-Louise (Scout) and her brother Jem live with their father, Atticus, and their cook, Calpurnia, in Maycomb County, Alabama. It is the 1930s, and prejudice, both racial and class-conscious, rages strongly. While Atticus practices criminal law the children spend their time at school and at play with their friend Dill. Their favourite game involves acting out the life of Arthur (Boo) Radley, a neighbour who has been shut away for so long that superstition surrounds him. As the game progresses (with Atticus' disapproval) it becomes apparent that it is not going unnoticed by someone on the Radley estate. During a night visit to the house, Jem loses his trousers: when he collects them they have been folded and inexpertly darned. Small gifts are left in the knot-hole of a Radley oak, until Boo's brother – claiming that the tree is dying – fills the hole with cement.

Who? What? Why? When? Where? How?

1. The hanging of Atticus' first two clients. Had they agreed to plead Guilty to second-degree murder he could have saved them, but they refused (1)
2. Meridian, Mississippi. His aunt, Miss Rachel Haverford, lives in Maycomb (1)
3. They kept themselves to themselves; they did not go to church (1)
4. As a disgrace. Mr Radley 'bought' his son's release with a promise to keep him out of trouble: Arthur was not seen again for 15 years (1)
5. Read and write. She cannot remember learning to read (it came to her as naturally as 'breathing'); Calpurnia taught her to write (2)
6. The Ewells. None of them worked; they lived like animals; none of the children had an education; their father was an alcoholic (8)
7. As a child who always spoke nicely to her (5)
8. 'A Negro' (but really at Jem, Scout and Dill) (6)
9. When Jem decides to go back to get his trousers. Scout does not understand that Jem is less frightened by the shotgun than by the thought of Atticus' disappointment in him (6)
10. Jem understands that it was Boo who left the gifts, and that his brother knew this and disapproved. He is angry at the lie, and at the frustration of their pleasurable discoveries. Perhaps he has started to feel sorry for Boo. (7)

Who is this?

1. Calpurnia (1)
2. Dill (Charles Baker Harris) (1)
3. Mr Radley (Arthur's father) (1)
4. The Cunninghams (2)
5. Atticus (5)
6. Miss Maudie Atkinson (5)
7. Atticus, of Arthur (Boo) Radley (5)
8. Jem (7)

Names and nicknames

1. According to neighbourhood legend and superstition the Radley place housed a 'malevolent phantom' who peeped in people's windows at night and committed 'stealthy crimes'. Arthur's history, and the mystery surrounding him, confers upon him this ghostly status. The name 'Boo' expresses this, and gives the children a familiarity with Arthur, and therefore lessens their very real fear
2. Something that is 'Attic' is of, or pertaining to, Athens. The characteristic Athenian qualities (in Ancient Greece) were refinement, elegance and classical purity – particularly in the art of speaking. The Ancient Greeks were notable 'orators'. To resolve their dispute Jem and Scout 'consulted' Atticus. The word is significant: what else do we 'consult'? They look up to their father, respecting his judgement, his fairness and his knowledge
3. It is a boyish nickname. Scout longs to be accepted and included in the boys' games, and Jem can get her to do (or not do) things by saying how much like 'a girl' she is becoming. Think about how this aspect of Scout allows her to participate more fully in the events of the novel, so that we 'see' them first-hand and through her eyes. Would it be the same if she were a 'ladylike' little girl? To 'scout about' is to look for something (often information). Is Scout inquisitive? Remember her love of reading anything she can get her hands on. In the military, a scout is someone sent on ahead to find out the position of the enemy. Do Jem and Dill ever use Scout like this?

Chapter 8

Mrs Radley dies. The children see snow for the first time. The winter is the coldest since 1885. The children make a snowman which is a caricature of Mr Avery (a 'morphodite' as Miss Maudie calls it). But Atticus, with his usual tact, makes them change its shape so as not to offend Mr Avery. While the children watch the fire which burns down Miss Maudie Atkinson's home, someone puts a blanket around Scout's shoulders. It is realised later that this must have been Boo Radley. For Jem, this act of kindness clinches Boo Radley's true nature and he pours out all their dealings with Boo to his father. Miss Maudie accepts the ruin of her home philosophically.

'Next morning I awoke...'

The snowfall results in different kinds of humour. Scout's behaviour is funny because she over-reacts out of ignorance; there is the narrator's dry humour about the effects of sin; then there is Scout's innocent trust in all adult pronouncements. (The information about the Rosetta Stone is, of course, nonsense; this Egyptian stone inscribed with hieroglyphics had nothing at all to do with weather prediction!)

'The telephone rang...'

The smallness of the town is emphasised here. Look at the list of jobs entrusted to the town's telephone operator. Touches like this are continual reminders of the inward-looking nature of this isolated town. It takes a man two days to get from the north end of the county to Maycomb in order to obtain 'store-bought' goods, which is perhaps surprising when we recall that Maycomb was the centre of government for the county.

'I looked down...'

What does Atticus mean when he says, 'Looks like all of Maycomb was out tonight, in one way or another...'? Jem realises who has put the blanket round Scout's shoulders – this is another example of real life contradicting the children's previously held beliefs. This happens several times: look, for example, at their meeting with Dolphus Raymond in Chapter 20.

Why is Jem so anxious to tell Atticus all they know about Boo Radley? What does Jem now realise about Boo's character that Scout has yet to appreciate? To identify how she still sees him, study Scout's reaction when Jem mimics Boo approaching her with the blanket.

"Don't you worry about me..."

Miss Maudie's reaction to the destruction of her home tells you about her character. Why do you think Scout is surprised at her reaction? Miss Maudie seems to care more for her flowers than for her home, but in fact this is quite in keeping with her character. These are the things which she regards as most important in life. Can you explain why the loss of her house does not upset her more than it does?

Chapter 9

Atticus knows that defending Tom Robinson will have a deep effect on his family. He already sees this with Scout; he has to persuade her not to let it bother her when people insult him. Uncle Jack (Atticus' brother) arrives for Christmas and Jem and Scout get air-rifles from Atticus. They all go to Finch's Landing for Christmas Day. Scout manages to control her behaviour until she meets her cousin Francis, but he provokes her into a fight with him. She is punished by Uncle Jack – unjustly, she feels, because her side of things has not been heard. When the children have gone to bed, Atticus explains to his brother that he is worried that Scout will not be able to cope with the pressure put on the family while he is defending Tom Robinson. During this conversation, Atticus knows that Scout (who came down for a drink of water) is listening from the hall.

"You can just take..."

The trial is introduced from Scout's point of view. Scout's frankness is funny. After her father's vain attempts to control her spirited behaviour she admits: 'I soon forgot'. For a young hothead like Scout, Atticus' lessons on tolerance fail to go very deep.

"Because I could never..."

The case of Tom Robinson is a matter of honour for Atticus. He knows he cannot win, but he must take it on or lose his self-respect, the respect of his children and the respect of those townsfolk whose opinions he values.

Unlike the Boo Radley story, where mystery and suspense are important elements, there is little suspense about the outcome of the Robinson trial. The narrator lets you know from the beginning the likely result. What effect does this produce, and what is your attention held by, if not the outcome of the trial?

Tom Robinson, the Negro accused of raping **Mayella Ewell**, is a married man who becomes a victim of the society in which he lives. Although he has a criminal record and has served a prison sentence in the past, he is a respectable, honest family man who gets into trouble simply because he feels sorry for a white woman. It is proved that he could not have attacked anyone in the way his accusers describe, because of his withered arm. But he is found guilty because people cannot bring themselves to accept the fact that a white woman desired a black man. Chapter 19 describes Tom's fatal error and the reaction of others to it.

In many ways, Tom is like Boo Radley – things happen to him, but he remains a mystery. Look at Chapter 19 and see if you can work out what Tom may have been thinking from the time when he approached the Ewell's place on 21 November (the date of the alleged rape) to when he ran away from Bob Ewell.

"Atticus, are we going to win it?"

Justice

Atticus is certain he will lose the case because he knows exactly what the status of the Negro is in the South. In spite of the abolition of slavery at the end of the Civil War, Southern Negroes remained second-class citizens. They lived in a separate part of town, received inferior education, and had to take on the poorly paid jobs. Even in court they were not equal. This is why Atticus is so sure of failure.

"Come here, Scout..."

Atticus

Courage

Scout is beginning to remember to be reasonable, and for a few weeks she accepts being called a coward for the sake of her father. She is starting to grow up.

Atticus has a great sense of duty towards his family. He refuses to break the tradition of Christmas, even if some members of the family are tiresome to be with. This is important, because it demonstrates that even the tolerant Atticus has to work at keeping his feelings under control.

An important lesson that the children learn as they get older is that adults frequently have to do things which they would rather not do (for all kinds of reasons), and that they must do them properly. Examples of this are: persevering in the face of defeat; exposing liars; shooting dogs; visiting dull relatives. These are all done by Atticus. See if you can identify who, as part of their increasing adulthood, has to: read to a viperous old lady; wear skirts; be polite; outgrow irrational fear; not use fists to settle arguments; break with the lynch mob; and accept her brother's courage (no, this last one is *not* Scout).

None of these are applicable to Dill. See if you can find any examples for him. What conclusions can you draw from what you find for Dill?

'Rose Aylmer was...'

Atticus

Scout's growing-up process leads her into the use of swear words. Atticus wisely ignores this latest trend as a passing fad, and it is her uncle who reprimands her. Atticus' tolerant attitude towards his children comes in for a lot of criticism from the family, especially from Aunt Alexandra. Do you think Atticus is right to adopt the approach he does, or is he simply being a poor father and spoiling his children?

'Aunt Alexandra was fanatical...'

Scout

Scout is a tomboy. If Jem wishes to insult her, he accuses her of behaving like a girl – as in Chapters 4 and 6. There is a vast difference between Atticus and Aunt Alexandra in their attitudes to Scout. Atticus lets Scout be as she is. Alexandra tries to make her dress and play as a girl, mistakenly believing that Atticus would somehow secretly prefer Scout to be that way.

"If Uncle Atticus lets..."

Justice

Why did Scout attack Francis if she did not know the meaning of what he said? Most children have a well-developed sense of fairness and Scout is angry with her uncle, not for the beating but because he did not take the trouble to listen to her side as well. Scout has come to expect fair dealings because that is how Atticus has always treated his children. Contrast Scout's behaviour with that of Uncle Jack – the humour here comes from the way Scout seems to be telling him off. What has happened here to the usual positions of child and adult? Where else in the novel does this occur? (Look at the school scenes.)

"Jack! When a child asks..."

Atticus

Atticus understands children well. Firstly, he believes in honesty, because children know when they are not getting a straight answer. Secondly, he selects from their behaviour the things that need correcting (like Scout's hot-headedness) and ignores those things that are probably best ignored (like Scout's new-found interest in swearing).

"That's not the answer..."

Atticus

Atticus deliberately switches the conversation to the trial when he becomes aware that Scout is listening. This is because he wants her to hear what he is saying, and to think that she is overhearing it, rather than being told it directly. Atticus is clever here: you already know that Scout 'soon forgot' when he told her directly to do things. What is Atticus worried about? Read carefully his conversation with his brother to help you work this out.

"It couldn't be worse, Jack."

Courage

Atticus sets himself apart from the people of Maycomb. He does not share their prejudice when it comes to Negroes, and he is realistic about his chances of changing their attitudes. He is afraid that this trial might damage his relationship with his children. Whose influence does he fear they may fall under? What does he mean by 'Maycomb's usual disease'?

Chapter 10

The children explain that they are disappointed with their father's accomplishments compared to those of their friends' fathers. By the end of the chapter, they feel deep pride and admiration for him. Atticus shows courage and skill in shooting the mad dog. In this chapter, Atticus mentions the mockingbird. He explains that it is wrong to kill something that does no harm, and gives only pleasure with its song.

'When he gave us our air rifles...'

Atticus

Look at Miss Maudie's description of the mockingbird. As you learn more about the characters of Tom Robinson and Boo Radley, see how far you think they fit this description.

Why is talk of Atticus' limitations included at this point in the book? Does it diminish or increase his stature in the eyes of the children? How do the children eventually come to regard him?

Jem

'The rifle cracked'

Jem was paralysed by the marksmanship of his father. Why do you think Atticus had kept his marksmanship a secret? Atticus is no longer proud of something which, when he was younger, he was extremely proud of. Jem cannot understand this immediately, but realises later that as

Scout

people grow up their views of things change, provided they keep an open and tolerant mind.

Scout's reaction is the very reason why Atticus kept quiet about his skill with a gun. He did not want his children boasting about his ability to kill. In contrast to Scout, Jem is mature enough to admire Atticus' silence.

Chapter 11

Acting quite out of character, Jem loses his temper with the outspoken, cantankerous old neighbour, Mrs Dubose. In retaliation for the names she calls Atticus, Jem knocks off the heads of her camellias. Atticus is angry at Jem's behaviour. As punishment, Jem has to read to her for a month. Scout goes with him and realises that these reading sessions increase daily in length. When Mrs Dubose dies, Atticus explains the important part Jem and Scout have played in helping her overcome her morphine addiction. He tries to show them that they have been witnessing true courage at work. Atticus has great admiration for Mrs Dubose, in spite of her rudeness. Atticus explains to Jem and Scout that true courage is a matter of facing up to a challenge and does not necessarily involve violence.

'Mrs Dubose lived alone ...'

Mrs Henry Lafayette Dubose is a neighbour of the Finches who frightens the children with her unkind remarks. She is introduced and then dies in the space of one chapter, and through her the children learn an important lesson about courage. Over the years she has become addicted to morphine, which she used as a painkiller because of illness, but she struggled at the end of her life to free herself from the addiction, even though she knew she was shortly to die. Without realising it, the children help her to achieve an important personal victory.

Courage

The children, in their uncomplicated way, have clear feelings about Mrs Dubose: 'Jem and I hated her'. However, she plays an important part in their growing up, and by the time of her death they realise it is wrong to judge others too quickly or too superficially. They might have admired Atticus for the wrong reasons if they had known about his skill with a gun. In the same way, they learn that people they might never dream of admiring can have admirable sides to their characters.

'Atticus pushed my head...'

Jem and Scout are going to have to learn that one has to do what is right whatever other people think. To do that sometimes requires considerable courage.

Atticus

Atticus tries to cool the children's indignation at hearing their father being called names. He tries to make them understand that such language reflects badly on the person who uses it, not on the person it is directed at. This is a difficult lesson for them to learn and later, when Mr Ewell spits in Atticus' face, the children are not the only ones to marvel at his cool reaction. Do you think that Atticus was really cool about it inside? Do you think Atticus ever experiences strong emotions? Or is it that he has strong emotions, but even stronger principles?

'Jem opened the box'

Atticus tries to show his children the true meaning of courage. Mrs Dubose knew she was facing a painful task in breaking her drug addiction, with little chance of success. Her courage lay in making the attempt. The fact that she succeeded is actually not all that important, it simply demonstrates that sometimes it is possible to win such battles. Was Mrs Dubose's victory a pointless one, do you think? And how courageous is Atticus in taking on the impossible defence of Tom Robinson? Do you think Atticus is simply being stubborn for the sake of some silly principle, when he knows it will not make any difference in the end?

Courage

Do you think **Atticus** is doing the right thing in defending **Tom Robinson**? Everybody except the children knows what the outcome of the trial will be. Decide whether you think Atticus is leading Tom on with false hopes. Would it be kinder to tell Tom that his case is hopeless? Is Tom Robinson's life being sacrificed just so that Atticus' conscience will feel better?

If you think Atticus is just indulging himself to impress everybody with how good a man he is, then what do you think Atticus *should* have done? Should Atticus, who has been appointed to defend a man in court, simply not bother just because that man is black? Wouldn't this be unfair, especially as it is revealed that both the Ewells are probably lying about the rape?

Self-test (Questions) Chapters 8–11

Uncover the plot

Delete two of the three alternatives given, to find the correct plot. Beware possible misconceptions and muddles.

For the first time since 1785/1885/1985 it snows in Maycomb County. During the night, Atticus'/Miss Maudie's/Mr Avery's house catches fire; for safety, Atticus sends Jem and Scout to stand in front of the Radley/Crawford/Dubose house and, while they watch the fire, Boo/Nathan/Mrs Radley slips a blanket round Scout's shoulders. The children learn that their father is defending a Negro in a simple/uninteresting/difficult case and suffer taunts from their fellows. At Christmas they go to Finch's Landing to visit their Aunt Alexandra, and Scout ignores/fights/admires her cousin Francis for calling Atticus a nigger-lover. As the situation deteriorates, Jem and Scout are reminded of their father's qualities when he saves Boo Radley/Stephanie Crawford/the neighbourhood from a mad dog by shooting it expertly and humanely – they were unaware of his shooting skills. They are tormented by Mrs Dubose, a sick neighbour, and Dill/Scout/Jem loses his head and ruins her camellias. As a result he is forced to read to her until shortly before her death, learning afterwards that with great courage she had fought and beaten her addiction to reading/camellias/morphine.

Who? What? Why When? Where? How?

1 Why does Atticus say he doesn't know if Jem will become and engineer, a lawyer, or a portrait painter?
2 What does Atticus rescue from Miss Maudie's house?
3 What main reason does Atticus give Scout for his decision to defend Tom Robinson?
4 Why does Francis spend each Christmas at Finch's Landing?
5 Who 'ain't fair', and why?
6 How did Atticus come to be given the Tom Robinson case?
7 Why is it a 'sin' to kill a mockingbird?
8 Why does Atticus no longer hunt?
9 When does Jem lose his temper?
10 According to Atticus, what is the one thing that doesn't abide by majority rule?

Who is this?

1 Who 'died of natural causes'?
2 Who 'gathered his meteorological statistics from the Rosetta Stone'?
3 Who is 'crazy, I reckon, like they say, but Atticus, I swear to God he ain't ever harmed us, he ain't ever hurt us…'?
4 Who are 'clean-living folks'?
5 Who 'wore a General Hood type of beard of which he was inordinately vain'?
6 Who 'was the most boring child I ever met'?
7 Who was 'just moseyin' along,…'?
8 Who 'was the bravest person I ever knew'?

Trouble is coming

In this section we have a sense of trouble 'building up' for Atticus and his family.

1 How does Atticus try to prepare Scout for what is coming? What does this confirm/reveal about him?
2 What antagonises Scout particularly when Francis calls her father a 'nigger-lover' (think about what she says to Uncle Jack in her room afterwards, and to Atticus when Jem is at Mrs Dubose's in Chapter 11)?
3 What further information is revealed in the discussion between Atticus and Uncle Jack at the end of Chapter 9? Do you think Scout understood the implications at that time? Why did Atticus want her 'to hear every word he said'?
4 What do you think is 'Maycomb's usual disease'?
5 Who is the first adult to insult Atticus?
6 While Jem is at Mrs Dubose's, what do Atticus' words to Scout about the Tom Robinson case reveal about what he believes? What does he hope Jem and Scout will do when it's all over?
7 Atticus and Mrs Dubose seem friendly when they are together, yet she says insulting things about him. Why, do you think? How does Atticus try to explain it to Jem?

Self-test (Answers) Chapters 8–11

Uncover the plot

For the first time since 1885 it snows in Maycomb County. During the night, Miss Maudie's house catches fire; for safety, Atticus sends Jem and Scout to stand in front of the Radley house and, while they watch the fire, Boo Radley slips a blanket round Scout's shoulders. The children learn that their father is defending a Negro in a difficult case and suffer taunts from their fellows. At Christmas they go to Finch's Landing to visit their Aunt Alexandra, and Scout fights her cousin Francis for calling Atticus a nigger-lover. As the situation deteriorates, Jem and Scout are reminded of their father's qualities when he saves the neighbourhood from a mad dog by shooting it expertly and humanely – they were unaware of his shooting skills. They are tormented by Mrs Dubose, a sick neighbour, and Jem loses his head and ruins her camellias. As a result he is forced to read to her until shortly before her death, learning afterwards that with great courage she had fought and beaten her addiction to morphine.

Who? What? Why When? Where? How?

1. Jem has constructed a snowman from hardly any snow, in a very good likeness of Mr Avery (8)
2. Miss Maudie's heavy oak rocking-chair – the thing she values most (8)
3. If he didn't, he could no longer respect himself (9)
4. His parents left him with his grandparents so they could 'pursue their own pleasures' (9)
5. Uncle Jack; he didn't listen to Scout's point of view before beating her (8)
6. The judge pointed at Atticus and said, 'You're It' (9)
7. Mockingbirds do no harm to anyone; they sing for people's pleasure (10)
8. He realised his skill gave him an unfair advantage over living things (10)
9. When Mrs Dubose says that Atticus 'laws for niggers' (11)
10. A person's conscience (11)

Who is this?

1. Mrs Radley (8)
2. Mr Heck Avery (8)
3. Boo Radley (8)
4. The Robinsons (9)
5. Cousin Ike Finch (9)
6. Francis (9)
7. Tim Johnson (10)
8. Mrs Dubose (11)

Trouble is coming

1. He tries to explain to her why he is doing what he is doing, and to get her to receive the taunts with dignity – to learn to keep her head, no matter what other people say or do. Atticus always 'practices what he preaches' to his children: he does his best to bring them up to be as fair-minded, as generous and as dignified as he is himself. He is gentle and affectionate with Scout, pitching his explanation at a level that she can comprehend and reassuring her (9)
2. 'The way Francis said it'. People use the term to 'label' Atticus, as something dirty and ugly. Atticus points out that it only reflects badly on them, showing them to be ignorant and narrow-minded (9, 11)
3. We learn how bad the case is going to be ('It couldn't be worse, Jack') for Atticus – and Tom. That is the Ewells, who are white, against Tom, a Negro, and that there is no evidence. Scout would not have understood all the implications of this, but she would have picked up how difficult things were going to be for her father and especially that she and Jem must not listen to the town but go to Atticus 'for the answers'. The lesson would have been all the more effective in that Scout was eavesdropping – children listen harder sometimes to what people are saying *about* them than *to* them! (9)
4. Racial prejudice (9)
5. Mrs Dubose (11)
6. That he believes Tom to be innocent, and he desperately wants to help him. He hopes Jem and Scout will look back at things and have some 'compassion' (does the use of this word signify that Atticus suspects what the outcome will be?) and understand why their father did what he did (11)
7. She is old, sick and in pain. This often makes people bitter and 'vicious'. She also has different views from Atticus, but can still like and respect him. Atticus tries to explain to Jem that her courage was more important than her prejudices. Notice Atticus' words about bravery: 'It's when you know you're licked before you begin but you begin anyway and you see it through no matter what.' Is Atticus showing this kind of bravery? (11)

Chapter 12

Jem is growing up and, to Scout's disappointment, is unwilling to play with her any more. While Atticus is away, Calpurnia takes the children to her church. It is a memorable experience for them. They meet hostility from one person, Lula, but the majority are welcoming. Scout attends the service with interest and notices many similarities with their own church. They learn more about the nature of Tom Robinson's alleged offence and the situation of his family. They also look upon Calpurnia with new interest, and they enquire about her background and her relationships with the other blacks. A collection is made in the church for Helen Robinson and her children. Calpurnia tells Scout that Tom Robinson is accused of raping Mayella Ewell. Aunt Alexandra arrives.

'Jem was twelve'

Jem is growing up, and Scout finds it difficult to accept the changes in him. He indicates that he does not want their relationship to continue as before. Jem is coming under pressure from his classmates. This is a small-scale example of the social pressure that exists in Maycomb. Isn't this how intolerance and prejudice begin? Notice how even the tomboy Scout eventually has to conform to society's insistence that she behave 'like a girl' and wear a skirt. How does she manage to rebel against this?

Jem

"What you up to, Miss Cal?"

Jem and Scout are made to feel unwelcome by Lula because they are white. What point is the author making here about racial prejudice in the South? Does it work only in one direction?

Scout watches what is going on in the church with curiosity, comparing and contrasting this service with those in the church she usually attends. She is free from preconceived ideas about a Negro church, and this is reflected in the fascinated way she describes it.

Prejudice

> **Scout the narrator** gradually reveals information about the **Tom Robinson case** as she discovers it. How successful is this gradual and casual revelation of events? Are there other ways in which the author could have told the facts? Try to think of some reasons why these other ways might have been better.

"He's just like our preacher..."

The children's innocence shines through here. They have not yet become aware of the existing racial prejudice that the South in general, and in

Maycomb in particular. Scout does not understand that in terms of status, all Negroes are regarded as being lower even than the Ewells. This visit to church marks an important point in the children's education. For the first time they understand that Calpurnia leads a 'double life'. From her they learn the important lesson that you cannot change people against their will.

Chapter 13

Aunt Alexandra comes to stay indefinitely because she feels that the children need feminine influence during their crucial years of growing up. She is obsessed with 'good breeding' and fits in well with the neighbours, but not with the children because she demands different standards of behaviour from those they are used to. Atticus is torn between being courteous to his sister and raising Scout and Jem as he sees fit. After one attempt to try and impose his sister's standards on the children, he gives up.

"Put my bag in..."

Scout finds it difficult to talk to her aunt and dislikes certain aspects of her character. Notice how the children 'exchanged glances'. But there is a new maturity in Scout's attitude towards her aunt's stay. How would you have expected her to have answered Atticus' question?

'When she settled in...'

What evidence is there that the author is mocking in her description of Aunt Alexandra? Look at the section containing the words 'let any moral come along and she would uphold it'. What overall impression do you get of Aunt Alexandra? Aunt Alexandra seems quite disagreeable at first with her 'riverboat, boarding school manners'. She attempts to make Scout more lady-like, curbs the children's freedom and refuses to allow them to mix with the Cunninghams because the latter lack the right 'background'. She is at odds with Atticus about the way he is raising the children and thoroughly disagrees with his defending Tom Robinson. Scout never understands her aunt's preoccupation with 'family' and 'heredity' – what Scout amusingly calls 'other tribal groups'. However, Aunt Alexandra mellows after the trial, when she sees what a strain the events are placing on her brother. Scout looks on her aunt with new respect when she sees her self-control at the missionary circle tea-party. Aunt Alexandra, in her turn, comes to regard Scout with more affection. She is particularly kind to Scout after Bob Ewell's attack.

Family

"Speak to your Cousin Lily..."

Family characteristics are considered important in Maycomb, and no one clings more to this belief than Aunt Alexandra. She is particularly proud of the Finch family background and feels that Jem and Scout should also be made to feel proud of it. Atticus sees things differently. His discomfort is shown by the way he keeps saying: 'She asked me to tell you'. What other signs are there that Atticus does not really share his sister's belief in living up to the family name? Scout and Jem are upset by the way Atticus is talking. In which way do they not want things to change?

Chapter 14

Having Aunt Alexandra living with the Finch family requires some adjustments, but Atticus has to refuse his sister's request to get rid of Calpurnia. Atticus has a high regard for their cook, and his sister's arrival does not change that. Scout dislikes Jem's new maturity, and when he tries to talk to her as though he were an adult she fights him with her fists. Sent to her room as a punishment, Scout is amazed to find Dill hiding under her bed. Jem shows that he has left childhood behind when he decides to tell Atticus of Dill's presence. Atticus is understanding and, after informing Dill's aunt, allows Dill to stay the night. Dill tells Scout that he is unwanted at home. Scout cannot conceive of anybody being in that situation because she is so sure of the affection of her father, her brother and Calpurnia.

"What's rape? I asked him..."

No doubt remembering what he told his brother (at the end of Chapter 9), Atticus answers Scout's question truthfully, although using difficult legal terminology. Scout pretends to understand his definition and moves on to another query. Scout's question about visiting Calpurnia shows us several things at once. Firstly, it shows how quick Aunt Alexandra is to impose her own views on her brother's household. This demonstrates the extent of her prejudice and intolerance. Secondly, it shows how quickly Scout responds to threats to Atticus' authority, emphasising Scout's youth and loyalty. Thirdly, it shows what a difficult position all this places Atticus in. He is not some superhuman figure who is able to be reasonable and fair because he is different from other people! His tolerance and lack of prejudice result in great strain. Doing the right thing frequently involves making a sacrifice, and all real sacrifices hurt.

"They've been fussing..."

Jem is beginning to understand things from an adult's point of view. He has some sense of the worry Atticus must be experiencing at the moment. Scout, who still sees the world very much as a child, has no idea that these undercurrents are present.

Why is Scout so resentful of the change in Jem? What does it show about Scout that she will not accept his new ways without protest?

'He had taken thirteen dollars...'

What part of their childhood code has Jem betrayed, according to Scout? Why did he tell his father? Look at his concern that Dill should let his mother know where he is. Jem is growing up fast, and is becoming keenly aware of the way adults react. He knows that whatever Dill's home background may really be like, his mother will probably be very worried by his sudden disappearance.

"I'm not scared..."

Look at the diplomatic way Atticus deals with Dill's unexpected arrival. He manages to be responsible, by informing Dill's aunt, without betraying the child's trust. The situation is managed by Atticus with humour and without anger.

Contrast Scout, who is sure of Atticus' and Jem's affection, with Dill, who has everything in the material sense but seems to be unwanted by his parents. Do you think this explains why Scout says that Dill 'preferred the magic of his own inventions'? Or is Dill's unhappy home background another one of these inventions? Why might Dill want to invent such a story?

Chapter 15

Dill is allowed to stay. The peace of summer is broken by troubled events. Scout fails to see the significance of these. Firstly Heck Tate, the sheriff, and some of Atticus'

friends advise him to give up Tom Robinson; they are worried about the possibility of Tom being lynched. Atticus refuses. A lynch mob from Sarum, bent on killing Tom, arrives at the jail – which Atticus is guarding. Unknown to Atticus, the children have also made their way to the jail because Jem is worried about Atticus' safety. Unwittingly, Scout diffuses the explosive situation by chatting innocently to Mr Cunningham (one of the mob). The men see sense and leave.

'It began one evening...'

Scout

The use of a child as narrator increases the tension in the story. The reader understands the danger Atticus is in, but Scout does not.

Did Jem really not hear his aunt? How does his attitude to the situation differ from that of his sister? Why is he afraid, and not Scout?

"Do you really think so?"

For the most part, we never get to know the people in Maycomb who are Atticus' friends and who support his actions. This increases our sense of Atticus' isolation. Why might the author have wanted to do this?

'Our father had a few...'

Prejudice

The fact that it is unusual that Atticus 'liked to walk' underlines the very puritanical, joyless view of life that most people hold in Maycomb. According to some people in Maycomb, flowers are not to be enjoyed because they are sinful. It also appears that people regard walking for pleasure a strange activity. Harper Lee ridicules this notion.

'In the midst of this strange...'

Scout

Why does Jem refuse to go home? He knows something about the present situation that Scout has failed to grasp. See if you can decide why Mr Cunningham calls off the lynch mob. How has Scout's innocent questioning brought him to his senses? Why does Scout begin to sweat?

How do we know that Scout still has not fully understood the situation? Look at Atticus' reaction after the men's cars have gone and compare it with Scout's question about whether or not they can now go home. What do you think Atticus might have been saying to Jem?

Humour plays a very large part in the book. Much of the novel deals with peaceful events in Maycomb, but these events often have a comic element and sense of fun. This forms a powerful contrast to the horror of **Tom Robinson's trial**. Humour relieves the tragic aspects of the story and adds a fresh and original touch to the narrative. It works on several levels. The descriptions of some of the characters are amusing – Judge Taylor eating his cigar, Misses Tutti and Frutti with their ear trumpet, Cousin Finch reminiscing in Chapter 9, and so on. The repartee between the children, and their innocent wonderings about the origin of babies is also very funny.

Another source of humour is **Scout** herself. Examples are: her ignorance of school procedures (such as when the teacher raps her over the hand); her lack of knowledge about adult behaviour and her misunderstanding of Miss Maudie's retort to Miss Crawford about Boo Radley (where Miss Maudie wonders whether Miss Crawford invited her peeping-tom into bed with her!). Scout's innocence leads her to behave in unexpected and therefore funny ways. The most outstanding example of this is when she completely misreads the seriousness of the lynch-mob situation and begins a friendly conversation with Mr Cunningham.

Harper Lee uses **satire** when criticising the education system and when gently mocking characters like Aunt Alexandra, who is so sure she is always right, and Mrs Merriweather, who is a hypocrite. **Atticus** uses humour, rather than anger, to point out to the children why their behaviour is wrong, or to take the tension out of an awkward situation, as when Dill is found under Scout's bed.

Chapter 16

It is not until they reach home that Scout understands the full danger and potential violence of the evening. Atticus tries to explain how people change when they are part of a mob so that men like Mr Cunningham, who are usually friendly, can become a threat. The next day all the people of Maycomb County attend the trial, acting as if they were going to a carnival rather than to see a man on trial for his life. Disobeying their father, the children go to the courtroom and find seats amongst the Negroes in their balcony, next to the Reverend Sykes. There they can witness the proceedings without being seen by Atticus.

'Everybody's appetite was...'

Courage

Although Mr BB Underwood is prejudiced against Negroes he believes it is the job of the law, and not the mob, to bring a person to justice. Hence his willingness to defend Atticus against attack. Mr BB Underwood, like Mrs Dubose, is a character who can be admired and condemned at the same time.

'Calpurnia was serving...'

Notice the different attitudes that Atticus and Aunt Alexandra have towards Calpurnia. Atticus respects and values Calpurnia. He speaks frankly in front of her because he sees her as part of the family. To Aunt Alexandra, Calpurnia is just a Negro, and therefore to admit in front of her that a white person is prejudiced against Negroes is just adding to their grievances.

"He might have hurt me"

Atticus' observation reflects a crucial theme of the book: it took a child, Scout, to remind the adult, Mr Cunningham, that he is still a human being. When he was made to remember that he is also a father and a friend, he saw the error of his behaviour. This episode highlights the way in which pressure from others can change a person's behaviour. Remember what Miss Maudie said about Atticus being the same at home as he is in public.

"You goin' to court this morning?"

How does Miss Maudie's attitude to the trial differ from that of the Maycomb population in general? What does it say about her sympathy for Tom Robinson and her sensitivity towards others?

Miss Crawford does not have the honesty to admit her true motives for going into town. Consider whether Miss Maudie's sarcasm is justified. If you think Miss Crawford is lying about her reasons for visiting town, why do you think she is being so hypocritical? If she is trying to deceive Miss Maudie, surely she can see that it doesn't work?

Miss Crawford is quite the opposite of Miss Maudie. She embodies the worst aspects of Maycomb people. She is bigoted, prejudiced, unkind and a gossip. She filled the children with wild notions about Boo Radley. She teases Scout unkindly at Aunt Alexandra's tea party.

'We held off until noon...'

Notice that this trial is described as a 'gala occasion' in Maycomb. The trial is being treated as a day's outing, with picnicking in the square before the event begins. What does it say about the attitude of white Southerners towards Negroes that they will turn out to witness this trial, which they know to be a foregone conclusion? Perhaps the Negroes have come hoping to see justice done. What are many of the white people hoping to see?

"They don't belong anywhere"

The depth of racial prejudice in Maycomb is emphasised in the account of Dolphus Raymond's life and the sad predicament of half-caste children. Given what we know already about the narrow and rigid views of the Southern whites, is Dolphus Raymond's exile from their community, even though voluntary, all that surprising? Considering the way Southern society treats them, how similar are the half-caste children and characters like Dolphus Raymond, Boo Radley and Mayella Ewell?

Prejudice

'We knew there was...'

Atticus

Scout finds out that Atticus had not chosen to defend Tom Robinson: he was appointed to do so. She is puzzled because, had she known this, it would have been a good excuse to use when people were taunting her. Why didn't Atticus mention this to the children? In what way does this make him a more courageous man? Re-read Atticus' conversation with his brother at the end of Chapter 9.

'The Coloured balcony ran...'

The narrator draws a very amusing picture of Judge Taylor, from the cleaning of his nails with his pocket knife, to the chewing and regurgitation of his cigars. Despite these habits, he is an astute and competent judge. He is another character whose nature is different from his appearance. The novel is full of such people: it is a central theme of the book that people should not be judged by external appearance. A civilised society depends upon everybody learning to recognise this simple fact. The children's admission to the balcony underlines their lack of prejudice, but it also solves some problems for the author. From the courtroom floor, Atticus cannot see the children. If he could, he would probably send them out of court. Why is their presence in the courtroom scenes essential for the success of the novel?

Justice

Chapter 17

Mr Tate testifies that on being summoned by Mr Ewell he found Mayella with injuries mainly to the right side of her face. Mr Tate also verifies that no doctor had been called. Mr Ewell testifies next, and stirs up the court by the crude language of his accusation. He shows his ignorance and stupidity and does not understand the implication of revealing that he is left-handed. Jem understands that a left-handed person would be likely to cause injuries to the right side of Mayella's face, rather than the left. Tom Robinson, being crippled in the left arm, would have found it extremely difficult to inflict Mayella's injuries.

'Jem's hand, which was resting...'

Scout

Again the older Scout recalls incidents and observations from her youth that she did not understand at the time. She misinterprets Jem's sudden excitement because she does not understand the necessity for calling a doctor in a rape case. Jem does, and this contrast in the children's responses draws our attention to this revealing piece of testimony.

'All the little man on...'

Prejudice

The only way that Mr Ewell is 'better' than his Negro neighbour is in the colour of his skin. This was the crux of the racial situation in the South at this time. A person's character did not matter – Tom Robinson is an exceptionally kind and respectable man – it is merely the pigment of a person's skin which is important.

"Yes? She was screaming?"

Notice the effect Mr Ewell's crude language has on the public in court. Why is there such an uproar? And why would Mr Ewell be pleased with this result, do you think? Bob Ewell is a drunkard, almost certainly a cruel father, and a liar. He is a poor farmer but, unlike the Cunninghams, he does not try to live with dignity; instead he lives on relief cheques issued by the State. His children are filthy and half-starved because he spends his relief money on drink. He is often violent towards his children, and is trying here to turn one particular bout of violence to his advantage by accusing Tom Robinson of rape.

Justice

"There has been a request..."

Who could Judge Taylor be talking about here? How much of the rape case do you think Scout understands? Once again, interest is heightened by the older Scout describing things that Scout the child cannot understand, but that the reader can. Judge Taylor rules his court with order and common sense, and although the outcome of the trial is unjust, neither he nor the court are open to criticism. Both are fair. The fault lies with the prejudice of the people, particularly those sitting on the jury. As Atticus says in his summing up (Chapter 20), the law can only function properly if the people allow it to, for 'a jury is only as sound as the men who make it up'. Scout wants to know why people like Miss Maudie never seem to get onto juries, because then she feels that

Justice

justice would be done. This reveals another type of prejudice – women were not allowed on juries at this time.

"You say you were at the window?"

How does Mr Ewell seem to you here? Can you believe what he says about his property? Do you think anyone actually believes him?

The narrator describes Mr Ewell with great sarcasm. Why is it funny to call him a 'fragrant gardenia'? Scout refers to him as a 'red little rooster'. Why is this image appropriate? Scout's main concern is that Mr Ewell gains an advantage over Atticus by carrying the sympathy of the crowd. Emotional appeal seems to sway the crowd, not common sense. Mr Ewell is left-handed. This detail, together with another fact which we learn about Tom Robinson, is suddenly produced at this stage. Why would knowing these things earlier have spoiled the book?

Chapter 18

Mayella Ewell testifies. A picture emerges of her impoverished life: Mr Ewell spends relief money on drink, and she and the children have to cut up old tyres for shoes in winter. Her evident loneliness leads us to feel sympathy for her. Although she will not admit it, it becomes clear that Mayella's father beats her. The weakness of her accusation against Tom Robinson is exposed when he reveals his withered left arm. Mayella is angry with Atticus because she feels that he has humiliated her in front of everyone and suggested that she is a liar. Mayella says that after doing a job for her, Tom Robinson followed her into the house and raped her. The way Mayella answers Atticus' questions suggests she is lying. Mr BB Underwood spots the children in the court-room.

'In Maycomb County, it was easy...'

Mayella has tried to rise above her squalid living conditions and has some dignity. When her lies are exposed by Atticus, it is the fact that she has betrayed herself that hurts her so much. Mr Ewell also betrays himself but, because he has only the false dignity of the arrogant, he does not care – in fact, he glories in it.

Judge Taylor's approach to Mayella is sympathetic, even if he does find her hard to cope with. Mayella is quite a pathetic figure. She is so unused to being treated with routine courtesy that she feels that Atticus must be making fun of her when he calls her 'ma'am'. What vision must Mayella have of her own situation if she thinks that Atticus is making fun of her for having no friends?

Prejudice

Mayella's deceit brings Tom Robinson to trial. Although perhaps she cannot be forgiven for this vicious lie, both Atticus and Scout feel sympathy for her because they know she is the victim of her father's cruelty. Scout senses that she must be very lonely. It is perhaps understandable that she responded to Tom Robinson's kindness. Mayella's position in white society is neatly summed up by Aunt Alexandra, who describes the family as 'trash'. In Chapter 19 Scout reflects that: Mayella 'was as sad...as what Jem called a mixed child: white people wouldn't have anything to do with her because she lived among pigs; Negroes wouldn't have anything to do with her because she was white'.

'When Atticus turned away...'

Atticus

Why is Atticus not triumphant at casting doubt on Mayella's testimony? Knowing his ability to put himself in other people's shoes, what do you think is Atticus' opinion of her? Is Atticus' reaction here similar to his reaction when he was obliged to shoot the mad dog?

Chapter 19

Tom Robinson testifies that he often did jobs for Mayella. On this particular occasion she asked him into the house and then made advances to him. When Bob Ewell saw Mayella through the window, Tom became frightened and ran away. Scout believes Tom's version of the story. The deep prejudice of the South is apparent: there is outrage when Tom admits to feeling sorry for Mayella. The 'impertinence' of his words stuns Mr Gilmer, for he feels that no White, however poor, wants or feels they deserve the pity of a Negro. Dill is upset by this attitude and Scout takes him out of the court, where they meet Dolphus Raymond.

"Tom, did you rape Mayella Ewell?"

Justice

The predicament that Tom found himself in when Bob Ewell saw him with Mayella sums up the position of the Negro in the prejudiced South. Whichever way he acted in this difficult situation, he would have seemed guilty in the eyes of white people. If he tried to defend himself against a white woman's advances the situation would be seen to be of his making, and therefore his fault. If he ran, as he did, it would be taken as an admission of guilt. He was in an impossible position.

'Atticus sat down'

Despite his casual manner, Judge Taylor is strict about the correct procedure. Link Deas had spoken out of turn, therefore he had to be called to order. Look at how Atticus reacts to the judge's outburst – he understands that there is a certain amount of acting in the judge's performance.

"Tried to help her, I says"

Prejudice

The inferiority of the Negro's position in the South is again underlined here. A Negro's status was so low that to show sympathy for a white person would be seen as gross impertinence. Negroes were not seen by Whites as people with feelings. The Whites treat Tom's pity for Mayella in the same way as they would treat the suggestion that a dumb animal could feel sorry for a human being. They regard it as an insulting suggestion. This explains Mr Gilmer's outrage at what Tom says.

'This was as much as I heard...'

Dill

There is a big difference in the sensitivity of Dill and Scout. Dill is disturbed by Mr Gilmer's tone. Scout's attitude can partly be explained by her greater 'experience' of court matters (she expects the prosecuting lawyer to be harsh). Nevertheless it is Dill, not Scout, who grasps the reality of the awful position that Tom Robinson is in.

Chapter 20

Outside the court, Dill and Scout talk to Mr Raymond. He reveals the secret of his drinking bag, and explains that because he breaks the rules of accepted behaviour it is easier for him – and for other people – if he pretends to be a social oddity. His faith lies in children who have not yet had their innocence tarnished by prejudice. He is glad that Dill has the sensitivity to understand 'the hell white people give coloured folks'. In summing up, Atticus explains why Mayella might have framed Tom Robinson. He pleads with the jury to weigh the evidence without prejudice, and reminds them that in law all people are equal.

'As Mr Dolphus Raymond was...'

Courage

Scout has accepted the stories about Mr Raymond and so she judges him at first by his reputation. Her opinion changes as she talks to him.

What do you think of Mr Raymond's behaviour? Is he merely feeding people's prejudice by pretending to be odd? Would he not be better to set both Blacks and Whites a good example by showing that 'normal' people can live in racial harmony? Do you think he has tried this, become disillusioned, and finds this masquerade easier for himself and for others? Although understandable, is Dolphus Raymond's solution essentially cowardly? Is his 'cowardice' only 'forgiveable' because it seems as though neither he nor anybody else has anything to lose by it?

"Then you just pretend you're...?"

Prejudice

Mr Raymond reveals his secret to the children because he respects their innocence. They might understand him, because they have not yet been contaminated by prejudice. Like Atticus, Mr Raymond represents the tolerant Southerner. He can see the 'hell white people give coloured folks'. He is not blinded by fear and hatred.

'Atticus was half-way through...'

Jem

Jem, who has followed the trial with understanding, is confident that Atticus will win. But he is basing his judgement only upon what has gone on in the courtroom – on the evidence which has been presented. Atticus knows that the jury's verdict will be based more upon what they brought into the courtroom with them – their preconceived attitudes, opinions, and their prejudice.

'Atticus paused, then he did something...'

Atticus

Scout's humorous remarks about Atticus' state of dress indicate the exceptional nature of this case. Atticus is making great efforts to convince the jury not only that Tom is innocent, but that they must defy their ingrained prejudice, and stand up for a black man against a white. Notice the tone of voice and the manner that Atticus adopts to accomplish this.

"What was the evidence of...?"

Justice

Atticus sums up the crux of the trial. The time-honoured, rigid code of behaviour has been broken, and broken by a white person. Atticus is trying to make the jury face this. They must have the courage to question their long-held beliefs. They must accept that the real world is not the way they have come to see it. Atticus puts his finger on the nub of the issue: all people are equal in law.

Chapter 21

Calpurnia arrives to say that the children are missing from home. The children's presence in the court is noticed and they are sent home. Atticus relents and allows them back after supper to hear the verdict. Jem is optimistic and, after a long time, the jury return with the result. Tom Robinson is found guilty.

'Calpurnia marched us home...'

This is another example of humour arising from Scout's innocence: she has no idea why Calpurnia thinks the trial is unsuitable for her, but is delighted that it is Jem who is getting into trouble for a change.

"Nobody's moved, hardly..."

Justice

The final comment about Judge Taylor's performance comes from a Negro. Reverend Sykes says that, 'he was mighty fair-minded', even leaning towards their side a little. In this way, it is emphasised that the law itself is not wrong, but people's interpretation of law sometimes is. The way people view justice is influenced a great deal by their prejudices.

'Jem smiled. "He's not supposed..." '

Jem

Jem is convinced that the evidence is clear-cut, and confident that the verdict will reflect this. His growing-up process is far from complete; he has still to learn about the complexities of human nature and their effect on human behaviour.

'But I must have been...'

Justice

Atticus

The atmosphere in the court is as still as a cold February morning, when even the mockingbird is quiet. With their verdict, the jury have killed the 'mockingbird', which is here a symbol not only of a gentle, harmless creature like Tom, but also of human values and justice itself. The jury do not value these fragile things.

The recalling of the mad dog incident says something about Atticus and the courage he has to summon up at this point. Why will Atticus need to be brave? Who does he have to face? What knowledge does he have to accept? (Bear in mind the consolation which Miss Maudie offers the children in the middle of Chapter 22.)

The Negroes stand up as Atticus passes. What does this say about the respect the Negroes have for him, even though the verdict went against Tom?

Self-test (Questions) Chapters 12–21

Uncover the plot

Delete two of the three alternatives given, to find the correct plot. Beware possible misconceptions and muddles.

Jem and Scout go to court/church/jail with Calpurnia. A collection is taken up for Helen/Mayella/Lula, Tom Robinson's wife, because she can no longer find work. On their return they find out that Aunt Alexandra has come to live with them: her presence in the house, and Jem's new found aggression/education/ maturity, make life uncomfortable/pleasant/unbearable for Scout. Dill runs away from Aunt Rachel/home/an animal show. Tom Robinson is moved to the Maycomb jail: a group of men, led by Heck Tate/Joshua St Clair/Walter Cunningham, tries to 'get at' him but the tense situation is resolved when Scout/ Jem/Dill innocently intervenes. The trial begins and Jem, Scout and Dill watch from the Negroes' balcony/cubby-hole/porch. Mayella Ewell and her father accuse Tom of having beaten Mayella and then raped her, hurting her badly on the left side/the right side/both sides of her face: Atticus makes it plain that the Negro, crippled in his left/his right/both arm(s), could not have inflicted the injuries, and suggests that her father beat her. Tom, Atticus' only/second/third witness, claims that Mayella attempted to beat/patronise/seduce him. Calpurnia fetches the children home, but they return for the verdict: guilty. As Atticus/Mr Gilmer/Judge Taylor leaves the court-room, all the Negroes stand as a gesture of respect.

Who? What? Why? When? Where? How?

1. Who is 'growin' up'?
2. Why won't people employ Helen Robinson?
3. How does Calpurnia speak in church? What explanation does she give?
4. With what is Aunt Alexandra preoccupied?
5. What does Aunt Alexandra try to persuade Atticus to do, and why?
6. How does Jem break their childhood code?
7. Why has Dill run away, and how does his home life compare with Scout's?
8. What is Atticus' 'dangerous question', and why is it dangerous?
9. Why is Scout's intervention at the jail more effective than Jem's?
10. What makes Dill cry?

Who is this?

1. Who says: 'It's not necessary to tell all you know…'?
2. Who is: 'Enamoured, upright, uncompromising…'?
3. Who is '…no patriot…'?
4. Whose 'Mutual defiance made them alike'?
5. Who 'don't have buttons'?
6. Who is '…a deep reader, a mighty deep reader'?
7. Who is '…the loneliest person in the world'?
8. Who is '…not a run-of-the-mill man,…'?

Brother Tom Robinson's trouble

1. With one exception, how do the Negroes treat Jem and Scout at First Purchase? Do you think this attitude has anything to do with Atticus?
2. What 3 things are different about the First Purchase service, in Scout's eyes?
3. Who will hire Helen Robinson at picking time? On which other occasion does the same person show his support of the Robinsons?
4. What is revealed about Calpurnia's education, and the education of Negroes in general?
5. What kind of life does Calpurnia lead? Compare her existence to that of Mayella Ewell (18), or the mixed children (16).

'It ain't right, Atticus.'

Tom Robinson's trial explores the central themes of justice, hypocrisy and prejudice.

1. From the conversation in court Scout realises Atticus had to defend Tom, whether he wanted to or not. Why has Atticus not used this fact in his own defence?
2. Do you think Judge Taylor is a good judge? Give reasons for your answer.
3. What turns the court-room crowd into a tense, murmuring crowd? Why?
4. While examining the witnesses, Atticus uses several tones of voice. List as many as you can. How would you describe his manner in court?
5. Do you agree with Scout's opinion of Tom (respectable, well-mannered)?
6. Do you find Mr Gilmer's examination of Tom upsetting, as Dill does? Do you agree with Scout that 'He's supposed to act that way…'?
7. According to Atticus, what are the great levellers? Is he proved right?
8. What image of Atticus returns to Scout as she waits for the verdict? Why?
9. How does Scout know, the moment the jury enters, that Tom has been convicted?
10. Tom has been convicted: Atticus has 'failed'. Why do the Negroes stand up in respect?

Self-test (Answers) Chapters 12–21

Uncover the plot

Jem and Scout go to church with Calpurnia. A collection is taken up for Helen, Tom Robinson's wife, because she can no longer find work. On their return they find out that Aunt Alexandra has come to live with them: her presence in the house, and Jem's new found maturity, make life uncomfortable for Scout. Dill runs away from home. Tom Robinson is moved to the Maycomb jail: a group of men, led by Walter Cunningham, tries to 'get at' him but the tense situation is resolved when Scout innocently intervenes. The trial begins and Jem, Scout and Dill watch from the Negroes' balcony. Mayella Ewell and her father accuse Tom of having beaten Mayella and then raped her, hurting her badly on the right side of her face: Atticus makes it plain that the Negro, crippled in his left arm, could not have inflicted the injuries, and suggests that her father beat her. Tom, Atticus' only witness, claims that Mayella attempted to seduce him. Calpurnia fetches the children home, but they return for the verdict: guilty. As Atticus leaves the court-room, all the Negroes stand as a gesture of respect.

Who? What? Why? When? Where? How?

1 Jem (12)
2 Because her husband Tom is charged with raping a white woman (12)
3 Like the other Negroes. It aggravates people to reveal the extent of your education. You can't change them unless they want to be changed, so you can only keep silent or 'talk their language' (12)
4 Heredity (13)
5 To sack Calpurnia. Perhaps just because *she* is there now, and feels Calpurnia is no longer needed… but there is a suggestion that she does not like the extent to which a Negro woman is trusted and even respected in Atticus' house (14)
6 By telling Atticus that Dill has run away (14)
7 Dill does not feel wanted or needed at home; his mother and stepfather spend no time with him. Scout has always felt needed, wanted and secure (14)
8 'Do you really think so?' It usually implies that he can show the person confronting him that they are wrong. (15)
9 Jem understands how serious the situation is, but only aggravates the men by squaring up to them. Scout's innocent friendliness completely disarms Walter Cunningham (15)
10 The 'simple hell people give other people'. His reaction is instinctive when confronted with harsh reality – injustice, hypocrisy, prejudice, cruelty (20)

Who is this?

1 Calpurnia (12)
2 Aunt Alexandria (12)
3 Sinkfield (13)
4 Jem and Atticus (15)
5 The Mennonites (16)
6 Atticus (16)
7 Mayella Ewell (19)
8 Atticus (20)

Brother Tom Robinson's trouble

1 With the exception of Lula, they are courteous, welcoming and friendly. This may be because of their respect for Atticus (12)
2 1 No 'ecclesiastical impedimenta' (no piano, organ, hymnbooks, programmes); 2 the sermon is 'individualised'; 3 Reverend Sykes counts the collection and no one leaves until it reaches the requisite amount (12)
3 Mr Link Deas; in the court-room (12, 19)
4 She has been taught to read by a white person, and has taught her son; only about four Negroes in First Purchase can read (12)
5 She leads a 'modest double life', acting like a Negro with other coloured folk, and showing her education around white folk. She fits in in both communities: Mayella or the mixed children are accepted in neither

'It ain't right, Atticus.'

1 Because it would imply that Atticus believed in Tom's guilt. Atticus has to defend Tom as best he can; it would be unprofessional not to (16)
2 He is eccentric, and seems to take his job casually, but he keeps a firm hold on the proceedings. He is also very learned (16)
3 Robert Ewell's declaration: 'I seen that black nigger yonder ruttin' on my Mayella!' The crude and emotive language arouses emotions and prejudices (17)
4 Dryly, genially, quietly, serenely, wearily, sharply, compassionately. Atticus is courteous and cordial, rarely raises his voice or shows strong emotion
5 Tom exhibits no cruel or violent tendencies, but is polite, respectful and courteous. His only mistake is to say that he felt sorry for Mayella
6 Mr Gilmer's job is to cross-examine Tom. He does not do it objectively and fairly, as Atticus cross-examines Mayella
7 Courts of justice
8 An image of Atticus standing in a deserted street in the winter. The image is one of isolation: Atticus is alone, the doors are shut
9 They don't look at Tom (21)
10 He has stood up for justice to the very best of his ability, against tremendous odds. He has stirred people up, and made them think. In this sense, Atticus has not failed – he has taken a great step forward for equality and justice (21)

Chapter 22

Jem is outraged at the verdict and Atticus does not attempt to shield him from his new-found awareness of the injustice of Maycomb people. The next day, the Negroes send gifts to show their appreciation of Atticus, and he is visibly moved. The majority of the neighbours accept the verdict without surprise and feel Atticus was foolish to defend Tom. It is left to Miss Maudie to show the children that there is a glimmer of hope because Atticus did effect a small change in the jury's behaviour – he made them take longer to reach a verdict. Dill is utterly disillusioned with people and he resolves to separate himself from them when he is older. Bob Ewell insults Atticus by spitting in his face, and threatens future trouble.

'It was Jem's turn to cry'

Atticus does not try to pretend otherwise to Jem that, in life, the just and right thing is not always done. Jem is devastated, but Atticus realises that he has got to learn the harsh realities of life. Atticus acknowledges that only children seem to have been moved by the injustice of the case. The adults' view is that there is nothing anyone can do to change matters.

'Miss Stephanie's nose quivered'

Notice the contrast in attitude between Miss Crawford and Miss Maudie. Miss Crawford disapproves of the children being in court, especially on the Coloured balcony. Miss Maudie treats the children no differently, and even bakes them cakes as a treat.

Contrast Miss Maudie's view of religion with that of the strict Baptists earlier in the book. To Miss Maudie, Christianity is about loving one's neighbour and treating people equally. She understands that at certain times in life a Christian is called upon to live up to these beliefs. She tries to give hope to Jem, by saying that there are good men in Maycomb who try to be true Christians. She also makes an interesting point about Judge Taylor. He deliberately appointed Atticus because he knew that Atticus would give Maycomb the best chance of seeing justice done. Do you think that real progress has been made, and that Aunt Maudie's optimism is justified?

Like Atticus, Miss Maudie is a realist and did not expect Atticus to win the case. But she sees signs for optimism in that at least he made the jury think for a long time. Because of his youth, Jem cannot accept this; he does not realise that ingrained attitudes and behaviour cannot be changed overnight.

"I think I'll be a clown..."

This is Dill's reaction to the injustice of the verdict. He is utterly disillusioned with people; he wants to separate himself from them and become a clown who laughs at them. Who else has made him feel disillusioned with people? Who does Jem have to fall back on to help him through this difficult time, that Dill does not have?

Chapter 23

Predictably, Atticus reacts calmly to being assaulted by Bob Ewell and dismisses the children's fears for his safety by making them look at the situation from Bob Ewell's point of view. But Scout and Jem are still worried. Aunt Alexandra feels that Atticus is too optimistic about Mr Ewell. Atticus explains to Jem that there can be no fairer system of justice until people's basic prejudices are changed, and that will not happen quickly. Atticus reveals that it was a Cunningham who caused the jury to take longer in making up its mind. Initially the Cunningham wanted Tom to be acquitted. Aunt Alexandra dismisses the Cunningham family as being inferior 'trash'. This makes Scout angry as she, unlike her Aunt, does not judge people by their social position. Scout also disagrees with Jem's deduction that there are four kinds of people. To Scout, people are just people.

'According to Miss Stephanie Crawford...'

Do you find Atticus' reaction to the assault predictable? Remember his advice to Scout, in the early part of Chapter 9. Do you think Atticus expected Mr Ewell to react the way he did?

The children are naturally worried for their father's safety, because they believe Mr Ewell's threats. Atticus' hatred of violence makes him refuse to use a gun. He tries to make the children look at the situation from Mr Ewell's point of view. He is being extraordinarily reasonable in saying he would rather Mr Ewell vent his anger on him than on Mayella. Why might Mr Ewell be angry with Mayella? Do future events prove Atticus right, or is his faith in the basic goodness of all men too great? For once, Aunt Alexandra's interpretation of human nature is more accurate than Atticus'.

"But lots of folks have..."

Jem has still to grasp the complexities of adult life. Atticus explains the flaws in the legal system, but Jem demands a simple, easy solution to them. He does not appreciate that laws can only be changed when enough people want them changed. Atticus warns Jem that things do not happen overnight. This echoes something Calpurnia said earlier when she was talking about the level of general education amongst black people, and their resistance to learning.

"Don't be silly, Jean-Louise..."

Family

Notice Aunt Alexandra's rigid views on 'background' again. The Cunninghams are not suitable for the Finches to associate with because of their inferior background; Aunt Alexandra calls them 'trash'. (Contrast this with Atticus' definition of trash in Chapter 27). Is Aunt Alexandra influenced more by social position or personal qualities in her judgement of others?

'Jem was rearranging the objects...'

Scout

In the depressing context of racial prejudice and social snobbery, the relationship between Jem and Scout makes a cheerful contrast. Scout is eager to say the right thing to please her brother, while he, developing a sense of maturity, tries to give her advice and consolation. Jem's amusing pride in the new hair on his chest shows that he is still a child at heart, while Scout's wry comment that it looks lovely (when in fact she can't see anything) is just as touching.

'Jem kicked off his shoes...'

Prejudice

Jem's attempt to explain people's behaviour by splitting them into four categories is criticised by Scout. She recognises the worth of people like the Cunninghams and explains their difference as merely the result of a lack of education. Jem believes that she is idealistic in thinking there is only one kind of people, and thinks she will eventually become disillusioned, like him. Which side of the debate do you agree with? Which side do you feel that Atticus would support?

Chapter 24

Aunt Alexandra holds a missionary tea and the ladies of Maycomb attend. They reveal their hypocrisy as they talk with sympathy about the poor Africans but with no sympathy for the local Negroes. Mrs Merriweather talks about the poverty of the Mrunas and about how she cannot understand the 'sulkiness of the darkies'. She also cannot understand why Atticus should want to defend one. Scout is puzzled and unimpressed by their insinuations and leading questions – which make her the butt of their amusement. She comments that she prefers the openness of men to the company of ladies. However, her opinion changes when she sees how Aunt Alexandra conquers her emotions on hearing of Tom's death and manages to continue normally in company. Atticus relates the events surrounding Tom's death in a matter-of-fact way which conveys little emotion; the only clue to his feelings is his comments that Tom had seventeen bullet holes in him and that 'they didn't have to shoot him that much'.

'I didn't know whether...'

There is a new maturity in Scout. She is learning to be considerate and put other people's feelings before her own. She is careful to keep her dress clean in order to spare Calpurnia work. She also sits with the ladies, even though such gatherings fill her with 'vague apprehension'. Scout does this purely because she senses that if she does so her aunt will be pleased.

'The ladies were cool...'

Scout realises that growing up takes a long time. She is embarrassed by her own frankness in revealing that she is still wearing her trousers under her dress! Miss Maudie, loyal to Scout, does not join in the laughter. But Miss Crawford shows her unkind nature by trying to get a laugh at Scout's expense by referring to the children's presence at Tom's trial.

"I said to him: 'Mr Everett,' I said..."

Can you make sense of the Maycomb ladies' sympathy for poor Africans when you consider their callous disregard for the Negroes in their own midst? They do not see their own hypocrisy, perhaps because it is easier to feel kinder towards people who are far away. Do we all tend to have over-simplified views of distant places and events? This might be because we do not have all the facts, and because our own situation and prejudices are less likely to be involved.

The Maycomb ladies expect the Negroes to forget about Tom Robinson and get on with their lives as usual. They are not prepared to allow black people any status at all, let alone equal status with themselves.

'Mrs Merriweather nodded wisely'

Although Scout does not understand who the ladies are referring to here, it is obvious to the reader that they mean Atticus. Far from appreciating that he was trying to ensure that Tom received justice, they interpret his actions as merely 'stirring up' the Negroes, and making them dissatisfied. Miss Maudie is angry with their criticism of Atticus and a moment of tension occurs in the room.

"His food doesn't stick..."

It is interesting to note the change in Aunt Alexandra. Her love for her brother and the knowledge of what it has cost him emotionally to go through with this case has separated her from the views and attitudes she would normally have shared with the other Maycomb ladies. Hence her gratitude to Miss Maudie for standing up for Atticus. She diverts the ladies from their topic of conversation by handing out the refreshments.

'But I was more at home...'

Although Scout has not fully understood the ladies' veiled comments about her father and the Negroes, she concludes that she prefers the frankness of male company to the hypocritical talk of the ladies. The author suggests their hypocrisy with the abrupt ending of this paragraph and the start of the next. The women seem to provide the word Scout is looking for to describe them, but they are talking about something else – the people in the North.

"Hypocrites, Mrs Perkins, born hypocrites..."

Prejudice

There is some truth in what the Maycomb ladies say here. Although the Northern states did not practise the same open policy of segregation in the South in the 1930s, Blacks were still treated as second-class citizens in terms of education and job opportunities, and they certainly did not mix in society with any degree of social freedom.

'Atticus leaned against...'

Family

Notice the effect the news of Tom's death has on Aunt Alexandra. Her concern for her brother has brought her to see the situation from his point of view, and she is very moved. Maybe she realises that 'background' – as Miss Maudie points out – is not merely a matter of coming from a 'good' family, but is more a matter of having the courage to try to do what is right, even if it flies in the face of social custom. Miss Maudie's definition does of course allow that it would be possible for a black family to have 'background', whereas Aunt Alexandra's definition would never allow such a possibility.

"Calpurnia's on an errand..."

Scout

Scout appreciates that part of being a lady, and a valuable part too, is the ability to hide one's feelings and act normally in company. Scout learnt this lesson when Atticus first asked her how she felt about Aunt Alexandra coming to stay with them. Scout's admiration for her aunt increases as she sees her pull herself together.

Chapter 25

Jem and Dill go with Atticus to break the news of Tom's death to Tom's wife, Helen. Dill likens her reaction to being trodden on by a giant. This echoes the scene at the beginning of the chapter when Jem admonishes Scout for treading on an insect. Tom's death is accepted in Maycomb without surprise. The people remain unmoved by a highly critical editorial in the local paper, in which BB Underwood is bitter about the needless killing of Tom. Scout awakens to the prejudice of Maycomb people and realises that Tom's case was lost 'the moment Mayella screamed'.

"Don't do that, Scout"

We see again the idea behind the mockingbird symbol; that it is wrong to kill creatures that do no harm. Jem prevents Scout from killing insects because, 'they don't bother you'. When Tom Robinson's wife is told of his death, she falls to the ground 'like a giant with a big foot just came along and stepped on her'. If white society is the giant, how accurate is this image?

'Maycomb was interested...'

Prejudice

Note how the people of Maycomb receive the news of Tom's death. The repetition of the word 'typical' demonstrates how easily they slot the death into their preconceived ideas about Negroes. As with the alleged rape, Tom's behaviour is interpreted to his disadvantage – no matter what he does, in their eyes he has no human dignity.

'Mr BB Underwood was at his...'

Notice the cynicism of the Maycomb people. They are unmoved by BB Underwood's impassioned editorial. They see it only as a ploy to get Mr Underwood's work published in a more prestigious paper! The image of the mockingbird is repeated in the editorial and underlines the wickedness of killing innocent creatures.

'How could this be so...'

Scout

Scout finally wakes up to the truth about the trial of Tom Robinson. Until now she has taken the events of the trial at face value and has been puzzled by the reactions of Jem and Dill. Now she understands why the whole affair is such a tragedy.

Chapter 26

Scout is growing up. She no longer fears the Radley Place and realises what a nuisance they must have been to Boo Radley. She is puzzled by the attitude of her teacher, Miss Gates, who condemns Hitler's persecution of Jews, but sees nothing wrong in Maycomb society's treatment of Negroes. Miss Gates feels that Tom's conviction will teach the blacks a lesson. Jem does not want to be reminded of the trial as he has not yet come to terms with his disillusionment about people.

'Perhaps Atticus was right...'

Scout

Although Scout is beginning to mature, it does not mean she understands or behaves entirely like an adult yet. She cannot understand the decision of the people of Maycomb, who have voted to re-elect Atticus to the state legislature, so she accepts the mystery without trying to unravel it. Can you understand why Atticus was re-elected? Wouldn't it be reasonable to expect that, after his 'lawing for niggers', the people of Maycomb would throw him out? Atticus' re-election is a sign that Miss Maudie's optimism for the future is not altogether without cause.

"Nothing, sir." I went away...

Prejudice

Scout becomes increasingly aware of people's basic hypocrisy in thinking about the world. We've seen how uncomfortable she felt in the company of the missionary ladies who pitied the African tribe of Mrunas. Now she is faced with the strange contrast between those who condemn the persecution of the Jews but do not condemn the treatment to which the Negroes in their own town are subjected.

Jem still has not been able to come to terms with the knowledge that people are not as good as he once imagined. Do you feel that Atticus has come to terms with this knowledge?

Chapter 27

Life begins to settle down after the trial and only three things of interest happen. Bob Ewell finds a job, but is sacked within a few days. He believes Atticus fixed it in some way. Judge Taylor meets an intruder in his house. Tom Robinson's wife Helen is harassed on the way to work by Bob Ewell, until Link Deas makes him stop. Aunt Alexandra senses that Bob Ewell has not yet finally got his revenge and she fears for the safety of their family. Atticus is not so pessimistic. Jem and Scout prepare for the Halloween pageant at school, an event which they attend, unescorted, at night.

'Aunt Alexandra was thriving'

The narrator gently satirises the attitudes of the Maycomb ladies. 'They had so little sense of family that the whole tribe was one big family' mocks the exaggerated importance that Maycomb people attach to family names. Would everybody in the South have been better off if, like the Mrunas, they could see themselves as belonging to 'one big family'?

'Maycomb was itself again'

The National Recovery Act was introduced by President Roosevelt, but was seen not to be helping the country to recover from the economic depression. It was therefore cancelled (repealed) by the Supreme Court (the nine old men).

'When Halloween came...'

The author's scene-setting and cautious tone create suspense. Atticus and Aunt Alexandra have decided not to go to the pageant, so the children will return home alone. Aunt Alexandra has a feeling something might happen.

Chapter 28

The children go to the Halloween pageant alone. The darkness and eeriness of the journey across the school yard is stressed. Cecil Jacobs gives them both a fright by jumping out on them. Scout is so humiliated when she misses her cue that she wants to wait until the audience has left before she and Jem set off home. On the way they are attacked by Bob Ewell, who tries to kill them. Jem is badly hurt. Scout is aware of the presence of a fourth person, who saves them and takes the injured Jem home. On their arrival Atticus summons the doctor, who announces that Jem has a broken elbow. Scout is incurious about the stranger on the porch and does not connect him with the fight. The sheriff, Heck Tate, arrives with the news that Bob Ewell has been found dead.

'Mrs Merriweather seemed to have...'

Jem is becoming tactful and diplomatic. He is rivalling his father in his ability to say the right thing at the right moment.

Scout is very incurious about the stranger on their porch. Of course, she does not yet know that it is Boo Radley. Her lack of interest is ironic, because for the last two years she has been anxious to see him.

Chapter 29

Scout tells Heck Tate what happened during the attack. Atticus' misjudgement of Bob Ewell is revealed. He did not imagine that Ewell would go to these lengths for revenge. While relating the events it suddenly dawns on Scout that the person who was present at the fight and who saved them was Boo Radley.

'Aunt Alexandra got up...'

A strong note of sympathy for Atticus is struck here. The attack on his children has affected him deeply, and now he has to endure the shock of Bob Ewell's death. Whom does he think has killed him? For one so wise, Atticus made a great error of judgement over Bob Ewell. He miscalculated the lengths to which Bob Ewell would go in search of his revenge. His faith in people has, in a sense, let him down. Do you agree with Heck Tate's view that, 'some kind of men you have to shoot before you can pay hidy (say hello) to 'em'?

'He was still leaning...'

Look at the description of Boo Radley. Although he is as pale as a ghost, he does not have any of the frightening characteristics with which the children once furnished him. He is not a rampaging monster of the night; in fact, he is very shy.

Chapter 30

Atticus mistakenly believes that Heck Tate is protecting Jem by insisting that Bob Ewell fell on his knife. In fact, Heck is trying to shield Boo Radley. Heck argues that it would be wrong to subject Mr Radley to publicity, and Atticus finally understands the sheriff's reasoning. Scout likens Boo Radley to a mockingbird. No proof of who killed Bob Ewell is given – evidence for its being either Boo or Jem is available for the reader to decide. Read this and the previous chapter carefully before coming to your own conclusion.

'Atticus walked to the corner...'

Atticus believes that Jem killed Bob Ewell, but he wants there to be no cover-up. He wants the facts dealt with fairly in a court of law. But he has made another serious error of judgement. As Heck Tate points out later, with his injured arm and his lack of weight Jem could not possibly have stabbed Bob Ewell. This is the second time that an injured arm has been used to show that someone could not have committed a crime against a member of the Ewell family.

"I never heard tell that it's..."

Who is the sheriff protecting by insisting that Bob Ewell fell on his knife? What are his arguments for not bringing Boo Radley into the limelight of a public courtroom? Do they spring from legal considerations, or from humanitarian considerations to do with understanding others' situations?

'Atticus sat looking at the floor...'

Scout understands the sheriff. She likens Boo Radley – an innocent figure who has only done good – to a mockingbird who does no harm but merely sings. The two strands of the story are linked within this one image, because Tom Robinson was also likened to a mockingbird.

Chapter 31

At Boo's request, Scout escorts him to see the sleeping Jem and then home. While thinking of Boo, she is reminded of their childish selfishness. They received gifts from him but gave nothing in return. In recalling the events of the past two years she is aware of her greater maturity and of how far she has been able to 'stand in others' shoes'.

'We came to the street-light...'

Notice how much Scout has grown up. She is ceasing to be the child who sees everything from a selfish point of view. She finally has taken Atticus' lesson to heart; as she comments: 'you never really know a man until you stand in his shoes and walk around in them'.

Self-test (Questions) Chapters 22–31

Uncover the plot

Delete two of the three alternatives given, to find the correct plot. Beware possible misconceptions and muddles.

The Negroes show their displeasure at/appreciation of/ignorance of what Atticus has tried to do by spitting at him/cursing him/sending him presents of food, but the humiliated Tom Robinson/Mayella Ewell/Bob Ewell spits at him and threatens him publicly. An appeal against/for/before Tom's conviction is planned, but Atticus arrives in the middle of one of Aunt Alexandra's missionary teas with the news that Tom has escaped/been lynched/been shot dead trying to escape from jail. Life in Maycomb seems to settle down, although after Bob Ewell finds and loses a job, Judge Taylor/Johnson/Gilmer is disturbed by a nocturnal visitor and Tom's wife Helen is persecuted by the Ewell family. Returning at night from a Halloween pageant, Jem and Scout are attacked. Bob Ewell/Cecil Jacobs/Boo Radley is discovered dead at the scene, and it is revealed that his killer was Jem/Boo Radley/Scout's costume, come to defend the children. The Sheriff persuades/fails to persuade/begs Atticus to pretend that Ewell fell on his knife, to save Boo from conviction/public anger/public attention.

Who? What? Why? When? Where? How?

1. What is Atticus' reaction to the Negroes' generosity?
2. Why does Miss Maudie give Jem a piece from the big cake?
3. Why do you think Judge Taylor named Atticus to defend Tom?
4. Who took considerable wearing down' before pronouncing Tom guilty? Why was this surprising?
5. When Miss Maudie says, 'His food doesn't stick going down, knows it?' to whom is she referring?
6. What is Maycomb's reaction to Tom's death?
7. Despite the verdict, Bob Ewell still harbours a grudge. Why?
8. What made the 'shiny clean line' on Scout's costume?
9. Why is Boo's skin so white?
10. What does Mr Tate mean when he says Atticus has been unable to 'put two and two together' for once?

Who says?

1. Who says: 'If there's just one kind of folks, why can't they get along?'
2. Who says: 'Don't you look at me, Link Deas, like I was dirt.'?
3. Who says: 'Because – he – is – trash, that's why you can't play with him'?
4. Who says: 'Good Lord... You're still standing'?
5. Who says: 'Well, it's be sort of like shootin' a mockingbird, wouldn't it?'

'Hypocrites, Mrs Perkins, born hypocrites...'

In this section Scout tries to understand hypocrisy in two episodes: the missionary tea, and Miss Gates' reaction to Hitler/Tom Robinson's conviction.

1. Mrs Merriweather is 'the most devout lady in Maycomb'. What does 'devout' mean here? Is its use ironic? What is revealed about Mrs Merriweather here?
2. What do you think concerns Mrs Merriweather and Mrs Farrow the most?
3. Who is angered by their conversation? Is her reaction surprising?
4. Why does Aunt Alexandra give Miss Maudie 'a look of pure gratitude', and why does Scout find this hard to understand?
5. Do you think it is a coincidence that Atticus arrives when he does with the news of Tom's death? What might the author intend by this timing of events?
6. Who would you include in Miss Maudie's 'handful of people in this town'?
7. What qualities do Miss Maudie and Aunt Alexandra show when they return in composure to the 'ladies'? What word does Scout use to describe her aunt?
8. 'Over here we don't believe in persecuting anybody.' Who says this?
9. What does Scout find hard to understand about Miss Gates?

To kill a mockingbird

1. Who do you think is the 'mockingbird' of the story? Why?
2. Why does Scout say to Atticus that letting people know the truth about Bob Ewell's death would be like 'shootin' a mockingbird'?
3. What do her words tell you about Scout?
4. Which characters do you think *would* 'kill a mockingbird'? (In some cases this may be clear-cut; others may be more difficult.)

Self-test (Answers) Chapters 22–31

Uncover the plot

The Negroes show their appreciation of what Atticus has tried to do by sending him presents of food, but the humiliated Bob Ewell spits at him and threatens him publicly. An appeal against Tom's conviction is planned, but Atticus arrives in the middle of one of Aunt Alexandra's missionary teas with the news that Tom has been shot dead trying to escape from jail. Life in Maycomb seems to settle down, although after Bob Ewell finds and loses a job, Judge Taylor is disturbed by a nocturnal visitor and Tom's widow Helen is persecuted by the Ewell family. Returning at night from a Halloween pageant, Jem and Scout are attacked. Bob Ewell is discovered dead at the scene, and it is revealed that his killer was Boo Radley, come to defend the children. The Sheriff persuades Atticus to pretend that Ewell fell on his knife, to save Boo from public attention.

Who? What? Why? When? Where? How?

1 His eyes fill with tears (22)
2 Jem is now 'grown up' in Miss Maudie's eyes (22)
3 He knew that Tom was innocent, and that Atticus' fairness and lack of prejudice would give Tom the best chance of acquittal (22)
4 A Cunningham; Walter Cunningham was the leader of the mob that tried to lynch Tom at the jail (23)
5 Atticus (24)
6 That his action was typical of a 'nigger': cowardly, thoughtless and unplanned (25)
7 He knows that few believed his testimony (27)
8 Bob Ewell's knife when he attacks her (28)
9 His skin has hardly ever seen the sun, because he so rarely goes out (29)
10 Atticus assumes that Jem killed Bob Ewell, and he does not want to be seen to 'cover up' his son's involvement (30)

Who says?

1 Jem (23)
2 Bob Ewell (27)
3 Aunt Alexandra (28)
4 Dr Reynolds (28)
5 Scout (30)

'Hypocrites, Mrs Perkins, born hypocrites...'

1 Pious, religious. Its use here is ironic: it implies that she holds *herself* up to be 'the most devout lady in Maycomb'. Mrs Merriweather makes a show of her Christian values but in doing so, reveals herself to be shallow, patronising and prejudiced (24)
2 Their own security and comfort (24)
3 Miss Maudie. No: she has shown herself to be direct, fair and honest throughout the novel's action, unafraid to speak her mind (24)
4 Aunt Alexandra is more conventional than Miss Maudie. She appreciates Maudie's support and defence of Atticus, and is relieved that Maudie has put a stop to the uncomfortable conversation. Scout has never thought the two women get on very well (24)
5 In the middle of this polite social gathering, Atticus arrives with proof of harsh reality. *This* is the result of hypocrisy, prejudice, cruelty and ignorance: seventeen bullet-holes in an innocent man. The ladies' superficial discussion of Tom's situation ('sulky' servants/maids/looks/chauffeurs) is laid bare, by news of Tom's violent death and his wife's devastation (24)
6 Some or all of the following: Atticus, Judge Taylor, Heck Tate, Link Deas, Miss Maudie herself, Aunt Alexandra, Mr Reynolds, Mr Raymond. (You may not agree, but make sure you have reasons for your decisions, based on evidence from the text.) Think too about Tom Robinson, and Calpurnia: what are their values, their manners? Do they too have humility, a sense of what is right and just? (24)
7 Courage, dignity, composure. A lady (24)
8 Scout's teacher, Miss Gates (26)
9 That Miss Gates is inconsistent: vehemently against Hitler's prejudice and persecution, yet satisfied with the verdict of Tom's trial (26)

To kill a mockingbird

1 Tom Robinson, who has done no harm yet ends up being shot. His good manners are perhaps like the 'music' of the mockingbird. Perhaps also Boo Radley: capable of great affection and generosity, he has been forced into seclusion
2 The public attention would be a kind of persecution for Boo
3 That she has understood the full implications of the situation and finally understands Boo's shyness
4 Think about who has been revealed as hypocritical, prejudiced, cruel, ignorant, narrow-minded. *Then* decide from the text whether they have more positive traits (a sense of 'fair play', a conscience, courage, the ability to learn from mistakes, etc.) Think about Aunt Alexandra, Walter Cunningham (Senior) and Mrs Dubose. Your reactions may be complicated and even inconsistent. Most of all, bear in mind the novel's humane and generous ending: ' "Atticus, he was real nice..."... "Most people are, Scout, when you finally see them." '

About Harper Lee

Nelle Harper Lee was born on 28 April 1926, in Monroeville, Alabama, in the south of the USA. She was the youngest of three children, and her father was a lawyer. She was educated at Oxford, and also read law at State University, Alabama, but six months before graduating in 1950 she left to go to New York, with the hope of becoming a writer.

With encouragement and financial help from her friends she gave up the job she had taken during the 1950s in New York (with Eastern Airlines as a reservation clerk), and concentrated on full-time writing. In 1957 her first manuscript was submitted for publication, but she was urged to rewrite it. For the next two and a half years she worked on it and finally it was published as *To Kill a Mockingbird* in 1960, when she was 34. The book met with instant success and within two years it had won four literary awards, including the Pulitzer Prize, and in 1962 was made into a film starring Gregory Peck. Since then Harper Lee has been a full-time writer, a contributor to *Vogue* and other journals.

Why was the book so popular? Its success was partly due to the topicality of the story. Negro civil rights was an issue that was slowly gaining support amongst whites in the 1960s. The appearance of the book coincided with this new awareness, and Atticus' struggle to help Tom Robinson struck a chord with many readers. The simple narrative style, linked with its tongue-in-cheek humour, also contributed to its popularity, as did the dramatic and moving plot. The main characters, too, were well-drawn, realistic and appealing. Their dignity, strength and warmth were attractive to the reader.

The value of *To Kill a Mockingbird* extends beyond the local setting of a small Southern town in the 1930s. Its theme of having the courage to face up to difficult problems is universal. It is just as relevant now as when Harper Lee wrote it.

Harper Lee returned to live in Monroeville, where she spends her time writing stories and magazine articles.

Writing an examination essay

Take the following to heart

- *Carefully study each of the questions set on a particular text* Make sure you understand what they are asking for so that you select the one you know most about.
- *Answer the question* Obvious, isn't it? But bitter experience shows that many students fail because they do not actually answer the question that has been set.
- *Answer all the question* Again, obvious, but so many students spend all their time answering just part of a question and ignoring the rest. This prevents you gaining marks for the parts left out.

The question

1. Read and understand every word of it. If it asks you to compare (the similarities) and/or contrast (the differences) between characters or events, then that is what you must do.
2. Underline all the key words and phrases that mention characters, events and themes, and all instructions as to what to do, e.g. compare, contrast, outline, comment, give an account, write about, show how/what/where.
3. Now write a short list of the things you have to do, one item under the other. A typical question will only have between two and five items at most for you to cope with.

Planning your answer

1. Look at each of the points you have identified from the question. Think about what you are going to say about each. Much of it will be pretty obvious, but if you think of any good ideas, jot them down before you forget them.
2. Decide in what order you are going to deal with the question's major points. Number them in sequence.
3. So far you have done some concentrated, thoughtful reading and written down maybe fifteen to twenty words. You know roughly what you are going to say in response to the question and in what order – if you do not, you have time to give serious thought to trying one of the other questions.

Putting pen to paper

The first sentences are important. Try to summarise your response to the question so the examiner has some idea of how you are going to approach it. Do not say 'I am going to write about the character of Macbeth and show how evil he was' but instead write 'Macbeth was a weak-willed, vicious traitor. Totally dominated by his "fiend-like queen" he deserved the epitaph "this dead butcher" – or did he?' Jump straight into the essay, do not nibble at its extremities for a page and a half. High marks will be gained by the candidate who can show he or she has a mind engaged with the text. Your personal response is rewarded – provided you are answering the question!

As you write your essay *constantly refer back to your list of points* and make sure you are actually responding to them.

How long should it be?

There is no 'correct' length. What you must do is answer the question set, fully and sensitively in the time allowed. Allocate time to each question according to the percentage of marks awarded of it.

How much quotation or paraphrase?

Use only that which is relevant and contributes to the quality and clarity of your answer. Padding is a waste of your time and gains not a single mark.